NOTARY PUBLIC GUIDEBOOK

FOR NORTH CAROLINA

**Ninth Edition
2004**

NOTARY PUBLIC GUIDEBOOK

FOR NORTH CAROLINA

**Ninth Edition
2004**

REVISED AND EDITED BY

THOMAS H. THORNBURG

Established in 1931, the Institute of Government provides training, advisory, and research services to public officials and others interested in the operation of state and local government in North Carolina. The Institute and the university's Master of Public Administration Program are the core activities of the School of Government at The University of North Carolina at Chapel Hill.

Each year approximately 14,000 public officials and others attend one or more of the more than 200 classes, seminars, and conferences offered by the Institute. Faculty members annually publish up to fifty books, bulletins, and other reference works related to state and local government. Each day that the General Assembly is in session, the Institute's *Daily Bulletin*, available in print and electronic format, reports on the day's activities for members of the legislature and others who need to follow the course of legislation. An extensive Web site (www.sog.unc.edu) provides access to publications and faculty research, course listings, program and service information, and links to other useful sites related to government.

Operating support for the School of Government's programs and activities comes from many sources, including state appropriations, local government membership dues, private contributions, publication sales, course fees, and service contracts. For more information about the School, the Institute, and the MPA program, visit the Web site or call (919) 966-5381.

Michael R. Smith, DEAN
Patricia A. Langelier, ASSOCIATE DEAN FOR OPERATIONS
Ann Cary Simpson, ASSOCIATE DEAN FOR DEVELOPMENT AND COMMUNICATIONS
Thomas H. Thornburg, SENIOR ASSOCIATE DEAN FOR PROGRAMS
Ted D. Zoller, ASSOCIATE DEAN FOR BUSINESS AND FINANCE

FACULTY

Gregory S. Allison	Richard D. Ducker	David W. Owens
Stephen Allred (on leave)	Robert L. Farb	William C. Rivenbark
David N. Ammons	Joseph S. Ferrell	John Rubin
A. Fleming Bell, II	Milton S. Heath Jr.	John L. Saxon
Frayda S. Bluestein	Cheryl Daniels Howell	Jessica Smith
Mark F. Botts	Joseph E. Hunt	Carl Stenberg
Phillip Boyle	Willow Jacobson	John B. Stephens
Joan G. Brannon	Robert P. Joyce	Vaughn Upshaw
Mary Maureen Brown	Diane Juffras	A. John Vogt
Anita R. Brown-Graham	David M. Lawrence	Aimee Wall
William A. Campbell	Janet Mason	Mark Weidemaier
Anne M. Dellinger	Laurie L. Mesibov	Richard Whisnant
Shea Riggsbee Denning	Jill D. Moore	Gordon P. Whitaker
James C. Drennan	Jonathan Morgan	

© 2004
School of Government   The University of North Carolina at Chapel Hill
First edition 1939. Ninth edition 2004
This publication is printed on permanent, acid-free paper in compliance with the North Carolina General Statutes.
Printed in the United States of America

08 07 06 05 04   6 5 4 3 2
ISBN 1-56011-436-3
Printed on recycled paper

CONTENTS

Certificate Forms of Acknowledgment and Proof   25

Short-Form Powers of Attorney   44

Wills   45

VI AFFIDAVITS   77

VII RESOURCES FOR NOTARIES   83

PREFACE

This is the ninth edition of the Institute of Government's *Notary Public Guidebook* and the first in two decades not authored by William A. Campbell. The first edition of this book, by Elmer R. Oettinger and Harry W. McGailliard, was published in 1939; the second edition, by Royal G. Shannonhouse and Willis Clifton Bumgarner, in 1956; the third, by Ann H. Phillips, in 1965; and the fourth, by J. Ritchie Leonard and Patrice Solberg, in 1977. The fifth (1984), sixth (1991), seventh (1995), and eighth (2000) editions were written by Campbell, and his work will remain the core of this publication for years to come. The Institute and notaries public throughout the state are indeed indebted to Campbell's contributions to the practice of notaries public during his career.

Rights of considerable consequence may depend on the correct performance of the notarial function. The notary cannot be expected to discover without help the laws, practices, and forms essential to the office and its performance. This book seeks to furnish that help by weaving law, forms, and practice into a brief, systematic, and convenient reference work, and it should also be of substantial value to registers of deeds, clerks of superior court, and practicing attorneys.

This edition substantially follows the eighth edition but includes updated text and forms and three new appendices: "Requirements Pertaining to Change in the Status of a Notary Public," "Notary Public Glossary," and "Frequently Asked Questions."

While writing this edition, we were given particularly valuable assistance by North Carolina Secretary of State Elaine F. Marshall's staff members Gayle Holder, Director of the Certification and Filing Division and Patty Holloway, Internal Systems Consultant, Land Records Section. Marvin Shelton of the Department of Transportation's Division of Motor Vehicles provided valuable assistance as well.

At the School of Government, my thanks go to Research Fellow Ingrid Johansen, who played the primary role in researching, revising, and updating the text as well as working with the Department of Secretary of State to incorporate its improvements. Thanks also to Carolyn Boggs, who coordinated our efforts with those of the Department of the Secretary of State; to Larina E. Ouiridi (a law clerk while a student at UNC Chapel Hill School of Law) and Tracy Strickland (a law clerk while a student at Wake Forest University School of Law), who provided early research for the new edition; and, finally, to our Publications Department staff, who edited and formatted the book.

THOMAS H. THORNBURG
SENIOR ASSOCIATE DEAN
Summer 2004

I
THE OFFICE

Introduction

The office of notary public can be traced to the early Roman Empire. In the seventeenth and eighteenth centuries, as merchants and shippers ventured far from local markets, the notarial function became especially important because commercial agreements entered into in distant places required acknowledgment in a manner that would be respected at home.[1] In 1777, the North Carolina General Assembly authorized the governor to appoint "from time to time . . . one or more persons, properly qualified, to act as notary or notaries at the different ports in this state."[2] The statute was amended in 1799 to allow notaries to be appointed in every North Carolina county.[3] Throughout North Carolina more than 164,000 persons now serve as notaries.[4]

All fifty states have notaries, but their manner of appointment, tenure of office, and powers and duties vary greatly from state to state. A North Carolina notary should never assume that he or she can do what a notary in another state can do; the powers and duties of a North Carolina notary are determined by North Carolina law.

---

1. For a more detailed history of notaries, see Lawrence G. Greene, LAW OF NOTARIES PUBLIC 1 (Legal Almanac Series No. 14, 2d rev. ed. 1967, ed. Dusan J. Djonovich and Robert Sperry); Edward M. John, JOHN'S AMERICAN NOTARY AND COMMISSIONER OF DEEDS MANUAL § 2 (6th ed. 1951, by Frederick H. Campbell). See 58 AM. JUR. 2d *Notaries Public* §§ 1–71 (2002) for additional background about notaries.

2. Laws of N.C., ch. 8, § 15 (1777).

3. Laws of N.C., ch. 15 (1799).

4. Interview with Internal Systems Consultant Patty Holloway, N.C. Department of the Secretary of State, in Raleigh, N.C., Jan. 29, 2004.

Appointment of Notaries

Power to appoint

Although formerly the governor appointed notaries in North Carolina,[5] current law assigns this power to the secretary of state, with the only limitation that the appointee meet the qualifications discussed below.[6] The number of notaries appointed in any county or in the entire state is not limited.

Qualifications for office

Both the North Carolina Constitution and the North Carolina General Statutes (hereinafter G.S.) impose qualifications for holding the office of notary. Because the office is a public one,[7] the provisions of Article VI, Section 8, of the state constitution apply. This section prohibits any person from holding office who has been (1) convicted of a felony under North Carolina or federal law, (2) convicted in another state of a felony if the crime would also be a felony had it been committed in North Carolina, (3) convicted of corruption or malpractice in any office, or (4) removed from any office by impeachment and not restored to the rights of citizenship as prescribed by law.[8] G.S. 10A-4(b) limits eligibility to persons eighteen years old or older who reside or work in North Carolina. As regards "work[ing] in North Carolina," the secretary of state's notary public section defines a regular place of work, business, or employment as a stationary office or work space where one spends all or some of one's working or business hours; in addition, the business at which the applicant works must have a North Carolina address. An applicant who resides in North Carolina is commissioned in the county of residence; an applicant who is a nonresident is commissioned in the county in North Carolina where he or she is employed.[9]

Under the dual-officeholding provisions of the North Carolina Constitution, a person serving as a notary is expressly authorized to hold concurrently another elective or appointive state or federal office.[10]

Application for appointment

To request the application form for appointment as a notary, visit the local register of deeds or write to the following address: Notary Public Section, Department of Secretary of State, P.O. Box 29626, Raleigh, North Carolina 27626-0626. Applications may also be obtained online at the secretary of state's Web site, www.sosnc.com or www.secretary.state.nc.us/notary. The form requires the applicant to provide and certify the truthfulness of certain

---

5. Laws of N.C., ch. 8, § 15 (1777).

6. N.C. GEN. STAT. § 10A-4 (hereinafter G.S.).

7. *See* N.C. CONST. art. VI, § 9(2).

8. Article VI, Section 8, of the North Carolina Constitution also disqualifies persons for public office who "deny the being of Almighty God," but this disqualification is not enforced because it clearly violates the First Amendment of the United States Constitution. Torcasco v. Watkins, 367 U.S. 488 (1961); 41 N.C. Att'y Gen. Rep. 727 (1972).

9. Letter from North Carolina Attorney General to Elaine Perkinson (Mar. 23, 1994).

10. N.C. CONST. art. VI, § 9(2).

personal information, and it must contain no misstatement or omission of fact. An applicant should give his or her full legal name (no nicknames) on the application. An applicant may use initials for his or her middle name. A recommendation is required from a North Carolina elected official, and it must be contained on the application. A register of deeds who is the instructor of the course discussed in the next section may sign the application at the course's conclusion and thereby fulfill this requirement. An instructor must never act as the notary on any application for a student in his or her class. If the instructor is a register of deeds or clerk of court, however, he or she may sign as the instructor *and* as the elected official in providing a recommendation for the notary applicant. The application must be completed in ink, signed by the applicant, and acknowledged before a person authorized to administer oaths.[11]

The applicant should return the completed application form with the recommendation and a check or money order for the statutory fee of $50.00, payable to the "Secretary of State of North Carolina."[12] This nonrefundable fee is required for the issuance of the commission.[13] The secretary of state's office does not furnish notarial stamps or seals.

The secretary of state may deny an application if the applicant:

1. has been convicted of a crime involving dishonesty or moral turpitude;
2. has been convicted of a felony and his or her rights have not been restored;
3. has had a notarial commission or other professional license revoked, suspended, or restricted by North Carolina or another state;
4. has engaged in official misconduct, whether or not disciplinary action resulted;
5. has knowingly used false or misleading advertising in which the applicant, as a notary, represented that the applicant had powers, duties, rights, or privileges that the applicant did not possess by law; or
6. is found by a court of this or any other state to have engaged in the unauthorized practice of law. [14]

Notarial instruction

Before the initial appointment, applicants must complete a course approved by the secretary of state in the duties of notaries. This course must contain from three to six hours of classroom instruction.[15] Approved courses are currently offered by all community colleges and technical institutes. Attorneys licensed to practice in North Carolina are exempt from this instructional

---

11. G.S. 10A-4(b)(5).
12. G.S. 10A-4.
13. *Id.*
14. *Id.* at (c).
15. *Id.* at (b)(3). To complete the notary's course of instruction, an applicant obviously must be literate, and the attorney general has so ruled [letter from North Carolina Attorney General to Ludelle Hatley (Jan. 7, 1987)], though literacy is not *statutorily* required.

requirement,[16] but before other applicants will be issued a commission, the secretary of state must have received the completed current application bearing the signature of the instructor and the date on which the course was successfully completed. These instructional requirements are waived for second and subsequent commissions.[17]

Before they are commissioned, all applicants (including attorneys) must also purchase and retain for reference purposes a manual approved by the secretary of state describing the duties and responsibilities of a notary.[18] This book, the Institute of Government's *Notary Public Guidebook for North Carolina*, is currently the approved manual and may be purchased from the Institute of Government's Publications Office at (919) 966-4119 or online at https://iogpubs.iog.unc.edu.

Issuance of commission

The notary section director in the Department of the Secretary of State attempts to verify the information provided in selected applications, and a commission will be denied if the director finds that the applicant has supplied inaccurate information. An incomplete application can lead to the denial of a commission and retention of the nonrefundable fee.[19] Unless the application is incomplete or inaccurate or unless an investigation reveals that an applicant is disqualified from serving as a notary, the secretary of state's policy is to issue a commission upon receiving the complete application showing that the applicant has successfully completed the training course.

Formal Induction

The secretary of state's office sends the newly appointed notary's commission, along with a transmittal letter, directly to the register of deeds of the county where the commission is issued.[20] A copy of the transmittal letter is sent by the secretary of state to the appointee as official notice that he or she has been named a notary. The appointee must then appear before the register of deeds in the county of commission on or after the effective date of the commission, as shown on the transmittal letter, to qualify for the commission by taking an oath of office. Notaries take the constitutional and statutory oaths prescribed for all public officers,[21] as well as the following oath of office:[22] "I, _____, do swear (or affirm) that I will well and truly execute the duties of the office of notary public according to the best of my skill and ability, according to law; so help me, God."[23] The notary must pay a $10.00 fee to the register who administered the oath.[24]

---

16. G.S. 10A-4(b)(3).
17. G.S. 10A-6.
18. G.S. 10A-4(b)(4).
19. G.S. 10A-4(b)(6).
20. G.S. 10A-8.
21. N.C. Const. art. VI, § 7; G.S. 11-7.
22. *See* G.S. 10A-8.
23. *See* G.S. 11-11 (General Oath).
24. G.S. 161-10(a)(17).

If the appointee does not appear before the register of deeds within ninety days of the effective date of the commission, the register returns the commission to the secretary of state, and the applicant must reapply for a commission, sending another application and fee.[25]

After taking the oath, the notary signs his or her name (exactly as it appears on the commission) in "The Record of Notaries Public" maintained by the register of deeds. This record contains the notary's name and signature, the effective date of the commission, its expiration date, and the date the oath was administered. Should the secretary of state ever revoke the commission, the revocation date will also be entered in this record. After the notary signs the book, the register of deeds delivers the notary's commission. The register then completes the certificate of qualification and returns it to the secretary of state. After receiving the certificate, the secretary of state enters the oath date on the official record of notaries (kept in the secretary's office) to verify the notary has qualified for office. The secretary of state's notary public section permits "The Record of Notaries Public" to be maintained in electronic format as long as the traditional handwritten signature of the notary public is legible.

A person issued a commission may not perform any of the duties of the office until he or she has appeared before the register of deeds of the county where commissioned and taken the oath of office.[26] Moreover, it is a criminal offense and grounds for removal from office for a notary to perform the duties of the office before taking, subscribing, and filing the oath of office.[27]

Tenure of Office

Effective period

A notary's commission is valid for the five-year period shown on the commission unless the commission is revoked.[28] The term of office begins on and includes the effective date of the commission and ends at midnight on the day preceding the fifth anniversary of the effective date. For example, if the effective date of the commission was May 5, 2002, the commission would expire at midnight on May 4, 2007. A notary's commission expiration date is printed on the commission certificate. A notary must always be mindful of this date, as an incorrect expiration date on a notarial certificate could invalidate the transaction contained in the certificate.

Recommissioning

Strictly speaking, notaries' commissions are not renewed. Each so-called renewal is a new appointment, and with each new appointment a notary must qualify again by taking the oath of office before continuing to perform the

---

25. G.S. 10A-8.

26. *See id.*

27. G.S. 14-229. One who acts officially without taking the oath of office is also subject to a $500 forfeiture. G.S. 128-5.

28. G.S. 10A-5.

duties of a notary. The same procedure must be followed as for the first appointment except that the course of instruction need not be taken again and the recommendation of an elected official is not required. The number of successive appointments that a notary may obtain has no limit.

The notary's commission states its expiration date. A notary should not apply for a new appointment until approximately four weeks before the current commission expires. The application, with a check for $50.00, should be sent to the following address: Notary Public Section, Department of the Secretary of State, P.O. Box 29626, Raleigh, North Carolina 27626-0626. Applications can be obtained online at www.sosnc.com or www.secretary.state.nc.us/notary.

Notaries sometimes mistakenly perform official acts after their commissions expire but before they are reappointed and take the oath for another term. This is a criminal offense.[29]

Change of status

Notaries who change their addresses or names or resign their commissions are required to notify the secretary of state.[30] Within thirty days of changing his or her address, a notary must notify the secretary of state by certified or registered mail of the old and new addresses. Within thirty days of changing his or her name, a notary must notify the secretary of state by completing the change of name form. The secretary then amends the old commission, issues the commission in the new name, and directs the notary to appear again before the register of deeds for administration of the oath. A name change and new commission require the purchase of a new seal. A notary who resigns his or her commission must notify the secretary of state by registered or certified mail, giving the effective date of resignation. A notary who no longer works or lives in North Carolina must resign his or her commission. If a notary changes his or her name *and* county of residence or employment at the same time, the notary must apply for reappointment and purchase a new stamp or seal. Appendix II contains more information on change-of-status requirements.

Premature termination of commission

A notary's office may be vacated during the term in three ways. First, the notary may submit a voluntary resignation to the secretary of state; his or her name is then removed from the roll of active notaries. Second, a court proceeding in the nature of quo warranto (quo warranto is an action whereby a person's rightful claim to hold an office is determined) can successfully challenge the notary's qualifications.[31] Third, the secretary of state may revoke the commission of any notary against whom a complaint is made if the secretary finds that the notary, in performing his or her duties, has not complied with state laws, and, specifically, the secretary may revoke a notary's commission if the notary failed to administer an oath or affirmation when per-

---

29. *See* G.S. 10A-12(a) and 14-229.
30. G.S. 10A-13.
31. G.S. 1-515.

forming a notarial act in which an oath or affirmation is required.[32] Revocations result most often when notaries have certified documents not acknowledged or proved in their presence. Commissions have also been revoked when notaries have allowed other persons to use their seals.

The notary public section director, with assistance from the investigator and the enforcement manager in the secretary of state's office, examines every complaint concerning notarial misconduct. The notary who is the subject of the complaint receives a copy of the complaint along with a request for a written response to the allegations. The notary's response is sent to the complainant, and the complainant may in turn respond. The director may then request additional information from either party or third parties. If the director determines that the complaint is unfounded, he or she dismisses it. If the complaint involves a criminal violation, the director refers it to the appropriate district attorney's office, which will then decide whether to prosecute the notary.

If the director finds that the allegations in the complaint are true, he or she makes a disciplinary recommendation to the notary public section's enforcement manager. The most common forms of disciplinary action include the following:

1. A letter of advice informing the notary of his or her improper action and the method for correcting the error
2. A written reprimand informing the notary of the investigation's findings and warning that future violations or neglect of duty will result in additional and more severe disciplinary action

Suspension and revocation of a notary commission are less common sanctions. These sanctions are typically imposed when a notary

1. is convicted of a felony while commissioned;
2. cannot be contacted for a response to a complaint; or
3. commits a criminal act while performing notarial duties.

A notary may make a written appeal of a suspension or revocation or other disciplinary measures to the secretary of state's appeals officer. The officer will either reverse or uphold the sanction. If the sanction is upheld, the notary may then appeal to the North Carolina Office of Administrative Hearings. The hearing and judicial-review provisions of the Administrative Procedure Act apply to these revocation proceedings.[33]

When a commission is revoked or suspended, both the notary and the register of deeds in the county in which the notary is commissioned receive a copy of the suspension or revocation order. The order becomes effective two days from the date of the letter. As described in the next section, the performance of notarial acts after a revocation or suspension is a criminal offense.[34]

---

32. G.S. 10A-13(d).
33. G.S. 150B-2(3), -3, and -23.
34. G.S. 10A-12(a).

Criminal offenses

The following actions are made crimes by the notary law:

1. Representing oneself to the public as a notary or performing notarial acts without a commission (Class 1 misdemeanor)[35]
2. Taking, while a notary, an acknowledgment or performing a verification or proof without personal knowledge or satisfactory evidence of the signer's identity (Class 2 misdemeanor)[36]
3. Taking, while a notary, an acknowledgment or performing a verification or proof knowing it to be false or fraudulent (Class I felony)[37]
4. Knowingly soliciting or coercing a notary to commit official misconduct (Class 1 misdemeanor)[38]

---

35. *Id.*
36. G.S. 10A-12(b).
37. G.S. 10A-12(c).
38. G.S. 10A-12(d).

II

GENERAL POWERS

Scope

A North Carolina notary may perform any of the following notarial acts:

1. Acknowledgments
2. Oaths and affirmations
3. Verifications or proofs[1]

An *acknowledgment* is an act "in which a notary certifies that a signer, whose identity is personally known to the notary or proven on the basis of satisfactory evidence, has admitted, in the notary's presence, having signed a document voluntarily."[2]

An *oath* or *affirmation* is an act "in which a notary certifies that a person made a vow or affirmation in the presence of the notary, with reference made to a Supreme Being for an oath and with no reference made to a Supreme Being for an affirmation."[3]

A *verification* or *proof* is an act "in which a notary certifies that a signer, whose identity is personally known to the notary or proven on the basis of satisfactory evidence, has, in the notary's presence, voluntarily signed a document and taken an oath or affirmation concerning the document."[4]

Limitations
Territory

A North Carolina notary may act outside his or her home county anywhere in North Carolina[5] and may take the acknowledgment or proof of any

---

1. N.C. GEN. STAT. § 10A-9(a) (hereinafter G.S.).
2. G.S. 10A-3(1).
3. G.S. 10A-3(5).
4. G.S. 10A-3(9).
5. G.S. 10A-5.

instrument permitted or required to be registered regardless of the county in this state where the subject matter of the transaction is located, and regardless of the residence, domicile, or citizenship of the persons who sign the instrument or for whose benefit the instrument is made.[6] North Carolina does not recognize acts of out-of-state notaries performed within this state.[7] For example, an attestation by a South Carolina notary while visiting in North Carolina is invalid, and so, too, is an official act by a North Carolina notary while in another state.

On the other hand, acts of a notary of another state properly performed within his or her home state are fully recognized insofar as they are within the powers given to notaries by North Carolina law;[8] thus an attestation by a South Carolina notary performed within South Carolina according to South Carolina law is valid in this state. If a notary of another state takes the proof or acknowledgment of an instrument and the instrument does not show the notary's seal or stamp and the expiration date of the notary's commission, then the county official before whom the notary qualified for office must certify that the notary was an acting notary at the time of this certificate and that the notary's signature is genuine. This officer's certificate must be under seal and must accompany the notary's certification of the instrument.[9]

A North Carolina notary may perform within this state, regarding a transaction to be made in another state, any notarial function that (a) is authorized by the law of that state and (b) is to be performed for some purpose that is proper within that state.

Practice of law

A notary who is not a licensed attorney may not practice law.[10] The practice of law includes, but is not *limited* to, the following, whether rendered with or without compensation: preparing or helping to prepare deeds, deeds of trust, mortgages, wills, or similar documents; abstracting or advising on titles to real or personal property; and giving opinions as to the legal rights of any person.[11] However, a notary as a private citizen may prepare deeds or other instruments for a transaction to which he or she is a party,[12] as well as notarial certificates to be executed by him- or herself as notary.

Although the "practice of law" encompasses a wide range of activities, a notary should be attentive to two particular areas in which confusion is likely to occur—real estate transactions and matters involving immigration. The practice-of-law issue as it relates to real estate transactions is of special concern to paralegals and others who work for attorneys of title companies. Recent ethics

---

6. G.S. 47-6.

7. *See* County Sav. Bank v. Tolbert, 192 N.C. 126, 133 S.E. 558 (1926).

8. G.S. 10A-9(d).

9. G.S. 47-2.2.

10. G.S. 84-4.

11. G.S. 84-2.1.

12. *See* State v. Pledger, 257 N.C. 634, 127 S.E.2d 337 (1962).

opinions issued by the North Carolina State Bar have raised some questions about the role lay people (including notaries public) may play in residential real estate closings. Opinions from 1999 and 2001 concluded that an attorney must be present at the closing conference for the purchase or refinancing of residential real estate,[13] but two opinions issued in 2002 revised that conclusion. A person who is not licensed as a lawyer may not "handle" a residential real estate closing because that involves elements of practicing law. However, a person who is not licensed as a lawyer (whether or not the person is working under a lawyer's supervision) may (1) present and identify the documents necessary to complete a real estate closing, direct the parties where to sign the documents, and ensure that the parties have properly executed the documents; and (2) receive and disburse closing funds.[14] A lawyer may delegate these ministerial tasks to a nonlawyer whom he or she is supervising.[15] Or, a person who has no relationship with the lawyer and who is not licensed to practice law may execute these limited administrative duties.[16] A lay person whose activities at a closing overstep these administrative boundaries, however, engages in risky behavior. Lay people should avoid performing any services that may appear to involve providing legal interpretation or giving legal advice. Specifically, engaging in any of the following activities in connection with a residential real estate transaction constitutes the unauthorized practice of law:

1. Providing abstracts or opinions on title to real property
2. Explaining the legal status of title to real property, or the legal effect of anything found in the chain of title, or of an item reported as an exception in a title insurance commitment
3. Giving advice about rights and responsibilities of parties—whether unsolicited or in response to a party's question or to resolve a dispute between the parties—under circumstances requiring the exercise of legal judgment or having implications for the parties' legal rights or obligations
4. Instructing a party to the transaction about alternative ways for taking title to the property or the legal consequences of taking title in a particular manner
5. Drafting legal documents for a party to the transaction or assisting a party in the completion of a legal document, or assisting the party in selecting a form legal document among several forms having different legal implications[17]

---

13. North Carolina State Bar, Formal Ethics Opinions 99-13, 2001-4, 2001-8. State Bar ethics opinions are available online at http://www.ncbar.com/index.asp.

14. N. C. State Bar, Formal Ethics Opinion 2002-9 and Authorized Practice Advisory Opinion 2002-1, both issued on January 24, 2003. These opinions are available at the State Bar's Web site at http://www.ncbar.com/index.asp.

15. N.C. State Bar, Formal Ethics Opinion 2002-9.

16. N.C. State Bar, Authorized Practice Advisory Opinion 2002-1.

17. N.C. State Bar, Formal Ethics Opinion 2002-9.

In the context of immigration matters, issues involving the practice of law arise essentially because of an unfortunate linguistic coincidence between English and Spanish. In Latin American countries, a *notario publico* is a state-appointed, private legal professional who has duties that are in important respects similar to those of a lawyer in the United States. Because of the similarity between the terms *notario publico* and *notary public*, concern exists that Latino immigrants may seek legal advice from notaries public, mistakenly believing that they are receiving advice from legal professionals. To avoid the inadvertent compromise of such a person's legal situation, as well as outright fraud, many states, including North Carolina, have placed restrictions on notaries' interactions with the immigrant community.

North Carolina law provides that notaries who are not licensed attorneys and who advertise notarial services in a language other than English must give conspicuous notice with the advertisement (either in writing or orally, depending on the medium of the advertisement), in English and the appropriate language, stating, as provided by statute: "I am not an attorney licensed to practice law in the state of North Carolina, and I may not give legal advice or accept fees for legal advice."[18] Notaries required to post this notice must also prominently post at their places of business a fee schedule in English and the non-English language in which they advertise.[19] In addition, notaries who are not licensed attorneys may not represent themselves as "immigration consultants" (unless they are recognized as such by the U.S. Board of Immigration Appeals).[20]

Named party and interested party

A notary is disqualified from performing the duties of the office in any case in which he or she is a signer of the document or is named in the document, except as a trustee in a deed of trust.[21] Additionally, a notary is disqualified from acting as a notary if he or she will receive directly from a transaction connected with the notarial act any commission, fee, right, title, interest, cash, property, or other consideration in excess of the notary fees specified in Chapter 10A, Section 10, of the North Carolina General Statutes.[22] Fees or other consideration for services rendered by a lawyer, real estate broker or salesperson, motor vehicle dealer, or banker are excluded for purposes of determining this disqualification.[23] Thus, essentially, if a notary will receive anything of value from the transaction over and above the notary fees (except for the services listed above), the notary is disqualified.

---

18. G.S. 10A-9(g).
19. G.S. 10A-9(j).
20. G.S. 10A-9(h).
21. G.S. 10A-9(c)(1).
22. G.S. 10A-9(c)(2).
23. *Id.*

While many laws have validated the acts of notaries who were interested in transactions,[24] most of these curative laws apply only to past transactions. Thus notaries should not perform official duties when they are "interested" parties to a transaction.

Preparation or probate of wills

A notary who is not also a licensed attorney may not prepare or aid in preparing a will for another person,[25] but may witness a will if he or she is a disinterested party. Because a notary is prohibited from notarizing a document of which he or she is a signer, however, the notary may act *either* as a disinterested witness or a notary, but not both.

Only the clerk of the superior court may probate wills.[26] The notary's role in the acknowledgment of ordinary attested wills and in the attestation of self-proved wills is discussed in Chapter IV.

Performance of marriage

A notary is not authorized to perform a marriage ceremony unless he or she is also an ordained minister or a magistrate.[27]

Judicial functions

While many notarial duties are quasi-judicial, a notary's powers are limited to those specifically granted by statute. Unless also a judicial officer, the notary has no power to issue warrants, summonses, or subpoenas or to try civil or criminal court cases (the power to administer oaths and take affidavits is discussed in Chapters V and VI).

---

24. G.S. 47-62–64, 47-92–95, and 47-100.
25. G.S. 84-4.
26. G.S. 31-17.
27. G.S. 51-1.

III

ATTESTATION

Requirements for Attestation

A notary public in North Carolina must attest his or her official acts by a clear and legible impression of his or her seal (or stamp), by his or her proper signature, by the readable appearance of his or her name, and by a statement of the expiration date of his or her commission.[1] If the notary's signature is legible, the signature serves as the readable appearance of the notary's name. If the notary's signature is illegible, then the notary's name must be typed, printed, or embossed near the signature, and the name in the seal serves this purpose.[2] A notary customarily supplies the date and place of attestation if this information does not appear elsewhere on the writing.

Omission of either the seal or the signature invalidates a notarial act.[3] Although numerous statutes validate the past acts of notaries from which seals were omitted,[4] notaries should not count on a future validation statute to correct their errors.

The seal or stamp

The notarial seal symbolizes the power given to the notary by the state. Past practice was to impress seals in wax attached to the paper, but the statute now calls for an impression or inked stamp directly on the document.[5] The presence of the seal on a writing raises a presumption that the writing was

---

1. N.C. Gen. Stat. § 10A-9(b) (hereinafter G.S.).

2. *Id.*

3. In *Tucker v. Interstate Life Ass'n*, 112 N.C. 796, 17 S.E. 532 (1893), the court held that an attempted verification of a pleading before a notary was ineffective because the notary did not affix his official seal. The strict necessity for the seal was not changed by *Peel v. Corey*, 196 N.C. 79, 144 S.E. 559 (1928), although the case is annotated under former North Carolina General Statute 10-9 to suggest that the requirement has been dropped. Presumably, the omission of the notary's signature would, like the omission of the seal, invalidate the notarial act.

4. G.S. 47-53, -53.1, -102, and -103.

5. *See* G.S. 10A-9(b)(3) and -11.

attested in the manner required by law by a notary.[6] The notary's seal will not, however, cure a certificate otherwise defective on its face.[7]

A North Carolina notary may use either a seal or a stamp in attesting official acts[8] (when using a stamp, the notary should be careful to place it on a blank space of the document so that it does not obscure any of the text). The seal or stamp should always be placed on the same page as the notary's signature and close to the signature and expiration date. It must contain the name of the notary exactly as the name appears on the commission, the county in which he or she was appointed and qualified, the words "North Carolina" or an appropriate abbreviation, and the words "Notary Public."[9] The impression must be distinct enough for this information to be reproducible by photographic means. The impression of a seal must be smudged (with carbon or similar material) before it can be reproduced photographically, and a notary must replace the seal when it no longer makes a reproducible impression.[10]

So that the device may be used for more than one term, the secretary of state advises against including the expiration date of the notary's commission on the face of the seal or stamp. It is permissible, however, for the stamp to contain a permanently imprinted expiration date. Or, a notary may use a stamp which was manufactured with a preprinted line for the expiration date and fill in that line on the document being notarized.[11] If the seal or stamp is stolen, the notary should notify the secretary of state and the register of deeds and sheriff of the county in which commissioned.

The signature

The notary's signature must be written exactly as it appears on the commission.[12] Thus the name in the seal or stamp and the signature must always match. Any initials used on the commission must be used in the signature. In the signature, no deviation from the name on the commission is acceptable. If a notary changes his or her name, Chapter 10A, Section 13(b), of the North Carolina General Statutes (hereinafter G.S.) requires that he or she submit a change of name form and purchase a seal with the new name (see "Change of status," in Chapter I).

Residence

Although commissioned for a specific county, a North Carolina notary may perform official acts anywhere within the state boundaries.[13] When a notary

---

6. *See* State v. Knight, 169 N.C. 333, 344, 85 S.E. 418, 424 (1915).
7. *See* McClure v. Crow, 196 N.C. 657, 146 S.E. 713 (1929).
8. G.S. 10A-11.
9. *Id.*
10. *Id.*
11. *Id.*
12. G.S. 10A-9(b)(1).
13. G.S. 10A-5.

acts outside his or her home county, the county name in the official seal will not match the county name in the certification. For example, if a Davidson County notary certifies a document in Rowan County, the certification will begin:

North Carolina
Rowan County

I, [name of notary], a Notary Public for Davidson County and North Carolina . . . .

The seal on the document will show, however, that the notary is commissioned in Davidson County, not in Rowan. Certificates with this difference are nonetheless valid.

A notary moving to another county during the term of the commission should continue using his or her present seal until the current commission expires. The secretary of state will issue the notary's next commission for the new county upon approval of a reappointment application, and the notary should then obtain a new seal or stamp.

Fees

A notary may charge $3.00 per signature for taking and certifying the acknowledgment of the execution of any instrument or writing, $3.00 per person for administering oaths or affirmations without a verification or proof, and $3.00 per signature for a verification or proof.[14]

Some fee collection, however, is restricted. For example, it is illegal for a notary to charge, either directly or indirectly, greater fees than those set by statute.[15] Whether a notary may charge for mileage traveled in order to notarize an instrument is unclear, but a literal reading of G.S. 138-2 indicates that he or she may not. Certain statutory provisions disallow notarial fees in specific situations: A notary who is "an officer, director, agent, or employee" of a bank may be charged with a misdemeanor if he or she receives a gift, fee, commission, or brokerage charge directly or indirectly, "on account of any transaction to which the bank is a party."[16] Any person in the business of lending money in the amount of $10,000 or less and licensed under the North Carolina Consumer Finance Act of 1961 "shall not collect or permit to be collected any notary fee in connection with any loan made."[17] When loan

---

14. G.S. 10A-10.

15. G.S. 138-2.

16. G.S. 53-86. This restriction does not apply to savings and loan associations. *See* G.S. 54B-156.

17. G.S. 53-177.

documents are notarized, notarial fees are borne by the lender so that the legal interest rate will not be exceeded through additional service charges. Violation of the Consumer Finance Act is a Class 1 misdemeanor and relieves the borrower of the obligation to repay the loan.[18]

Attesting Documents That Have to Be Authenticated

Some documents that a notary attests will have to be authenticated by the secretary of state under Article 34, Chapter 66 of the North Carolina General Statutes. Typically these are documents that are to be used in a transaction in another state or country. For example, documents relating to the adoption by North Carolina residents of a child who is a citizen of another country must be attested by the secretary of state. Notaries should take special care in attesting such documents because considerable inconvenience to all parties will result if the secretary of state is unable to authenticate the documents and must return them for re-attestation. The following requirements must be met before the secretary of state can authenticate a document:

1. All seals and signatures must be originals.
2. All dates must follow in chronological order on all certifications.
3. All acknowledgments to be authenticated must be in English or accompanied by a certified or notarized English translation.
4. Whenever a copy is used, it must include a statement that it is a true and accurate copy; the secretary of state requires that this statement be in a sworn affidavit.[19]

Liability

The violations of notarial duties that are criminal offenses are outlined in Chapter I. Only once has a suit against a North Carolina notary for negligence reached the appellate courts. In *Nelson v. Comer*, a notary certified the acknowledgment of the execution of a deed by a man who claimed to be the owner of the property transferred by the deed.[20] The notary did not ask the man for proof of identity and thus did not discover that he was an impostor. A couple who relied on the fraudulent deed in a later purchase of the property sued the notary for damages caused by his negligence in taking the acknowledgment. The notary was held not liable. The North Carolina Court of Appeals stated: "A public official, engaged in the performance of governmental duties involving the exercise of judgment and discretion, may not be

---

18. G.S. 53-166(c) and (d).
19. G.S. 66-273.
20. 21 N.C. App. 636, 205 S.E.2d 537 (1974).

held personally liable for mere negligence in respect thereto."[21] However, a notary whose "act, or failure to act, was corrupt or malicious or . . . outside of and beyond the scope of his duties" could be held personally liable for resulting harm.[22] Thus, for example, a notary who intentionally falsely certifies an acknowledgment may be held personally liable.

The *Nelson* case was decided before the enactment of the current provisions of G.S. Chapter 10A, which require a notary to obtain satisfactory evidence of the identity of the person whose signature the notary is acknowledging or proving. It is possible that, should a case similar to *Nelson* arise, a court would now rely on the statute regarding evidence of identity to hold that a notary who willfully disregarded that statute is liable in a civil action. In any event, notaries who carefully follow all of the statutory requirements are unlikely to find themselves in a position where they might have to rely on *Nelson*.

---

21. *Id.* at 638, 205 S.E.2d at 538.
22. *Id.*

IV

CERTIFICATION

Introduction

North Carolina law requires that many transactions be put in writing and made a matter of public record in order to give notice to anyone who may later do business with one of the parties to the transaction.[1] Many written instruments cannot be registered as public records until an authorized official, such as a notary public, certifies that the documents were executed properly.[2] Normally, a person executes a document by signing his or her name to it. However, if the person cannot write his or her name, North Carolina law recognizes his or her mark as a valid signature, and a mark may be either acknowledged or proved in the same manner as a signature.[3] Also, if the person is physically unable to write, someone else, with the person's consent and in the person's presence, may sign that person's name.[4] And anyone who is blind or otherwise visually handicapped within the meaning of North Carolina General Statute 111-11 (hereinafter G.S.), may use a signature facsimile, which must be registered in the office of the clerk of superior court in the county of the person's residence.[5]

The execution of a document may be certified in either of two ways.[6] In the usual way, the person signing the instrument appears before the notary and either signs it in the notary's presence or identifies an earlier signature as his or her own. This personal appearance is called acknowledgment; that term is also used to describe the notary's written certificate that the acknowledgment occurred.[7]

---

1. *See, e.g.*, N.C. Gen. Stat. §§ 47-18 and -20 (hereinafter G.S.).
2. G.S. 47-17.
3. Devereux v. McMahon, 108 N.C. 134, 142–43, 12 S.E. 902, 904-5 (1891).
4. Lee v. Parker, 171 N.C. 144, 150, 88 S.E. 217, 221 (1916).
5. G.S. 22A-1.
6. G.S. 47-17.
7. 1 Am. Jur. 2d *Acknowledgments* § 1 (1962).

In the second method of certification, a person other than the signer of the instrument appears before the notary and states under oath that (1) the one who signed the instrument signed it in the person's presence, or (2) the signer acknowledged to the person that he or she had signed the instrument, or (3) the person recognizes the signature of either the signer or a subscribing witness as genuine.[8] This procedure is called taking the proof of an instrument. These two means of certifying a written instrument—acknowledgment and proof— and the forms for each are explained in this chapter.

Acknowledgment

Procedure

To acknowledge a written instrument, a person must do the following:

1. Physically appear before the notary. The acknowledger's actual physical presence before the notary is essential to the validity of the acknowledgment.[9] An attempted acknowledgment by telephone, telegraph, mail, or any other means that does not bring the acknowledger physically before the notary is invalid.[10] And it is unethical for an attorney to file a document for public record when the attorney has personal knowledge that the acknowledger did not physically appear before the certifying notary.[11]

2. Be personally known to the notary or have his or her identity proven on the basis of satisfactory evidence. A notary has "personal knowledge of the identity" of a signer when the notary has been acquainted with the signer for a sufficient time to eliminate every reasonable doubt as to the identity claimed.[12] A notary may establish a signer's identity by "satisfactory evidence of identity" in one of two ways: (a) either the signer furnishes the notary with a current document issued by an agency of a federal or state government with the signer's photograph (for example, a driver's license) or (b) the signer is identified by a credible person who is personally known to the notary and who has personal knowledge of the signer's identity.[13] A question arises as to whether a "federal or state government" document from another country is acceptable to prove (a) above. The Notary Public Section of the Department of the Secretary of State has taken the position that such a document is acceptable, as long as it is official, currently valid, and includes the signer's photograph.[14]

---

8. G.S 47-12, -12.1, and -13.

9. G.S. 10A-3(1).

10. *See* Southern State Bank v. Sumner, 187 N.C. 762, 122 S.E. 848 (1924).

11. N.C. State Bar, Ethical Op. 720 (1970).

12. G.S. 10A-3(7).

13. G.S. 10A-3(8).

14. Conversation with Internal Systems Consultant Patty Holloway, N.C. Department of the Secretary of State, in Raleigh, N.C., March 2, 2004.

3. Sign the instrument in the presence of the notary or state to the notary that he or she voluntarily signed the instrument. Generally, the acknowledger signs the document in the presence of the notary; if a writing presented to a notary has already been signed, the notary must obtain an affirmative statement from the acknowledger that the signature is his or hers and that he or she voluntarily signed the instrument.

Failure to meet all of the conditions described in this section may invalidate the acknowledgment and may also subject the notary to revocation of his or her commission.

Acknowledgeable instruments

Any instrument or document may be acknowledged, including deeds, deeds of trust, leases, powers of attorney, assignments, releases, and affidavits concerning land titles or family history.[15] Deeds, contracts, and leases must be acknowledged or proved before they may be registered.[16]

Acknowledger

The person signing an instrument is the proper person to acknowledge its execution. Also, an instrument signed by a certain person may be acknowledged by that person's attorney in fact under a power of attorney if the power of attorney so provides.[17] An attorney in fact who signs an instrument for another person under a power of attorney is the proper acknowledger of the instrument.[18]

Order of acknowledgment

When an instrument has been signed by more than one person, the acknowledgments need not be made in the same order as the signatures, nor must the certificates of acknowledgment appear in any particular order. Furthermore, an instrument executed by several different persons may be acknowledged by each of them before the same notary or before different notaries at different times and in different places.

Proof of Execution

Procedure

To prove the execution of a written instrument, a person must

1. physically appear before the notary,
2. be personally known to the notary or prove his or her identity on the basis of satisfactory evidence,

---

15. *See* G.S. 47-1.
16. G.S. 47-17.
17. Cochran v. Linville Improvement Co., 127 N.C. 386, 393, 37 S.E. 496, 499 (1900).
18. *See* G.S. 47-43 and -43.1.

3. give his or her testimony under oath, and
4. sign the proof certificate.

The notary must adhere to provisions (1) and (2) as stringently for a proof of execution as for an acknowledgment (see previous section). For provision (3), although a notary must administer an oath whenever the execution of a document is proved, the statutes provide no specific oath. The following oath suffices:

Do you swear [or affirm] that the information you give concerning this writing is the truth, so help you, God?

The procedure for administering oaths as explained in Chapter V should be followed.

Notaries often do not administer oaths in situations that require them. Although the notary's certificate that the witness was duly sworn is presumptive evidence that the oath was given, questions concerning the validity of the certificate may be raised if the oath was omitted. Also, a certificate of proof that does not indicate that the person proving the instrument was placed under oath has no legal validity.[19]

Provable instruments

Ordinarily, the signing of any instrument that may be acknowledged may also be proved. However, the North Carolina Division of Motor Vehicles (DMV) requires that signatures on title documents be acknowledged rather than proved; if, therefore, a notary uses a proof of execution on a DMV document, the certification will be invalid.[20]

Proof taker

A notary public may take the proof of the signing of any writing that may be proved.[21]

Proof giver

1. *Subscribing witnesses.* The signing of an instrument may be proved by the sworn testimony of a subscribing witness to the instrument.[22] A subscribing witness is a witness who signed the document. The witness states under oath that the person who executed the instrument either signed it in the witness's presence or acknowledged its execution to him or her.[23] If, however, the subscribing witness is a

---

19. McClure v. Crow, 196 N.C. 657, 661, 146 S.E. 713, 715 (1929).
20. *See* G.S. 20-72.
21. G.S. 47-1.
22. G.S. 47-12.
23. *Id.*

grantee or beneficiary in the instrument, he or she may not prove the execution of the instrument, nor may his or her signature be proved by anyone else.[24]

2. *Other persons.* If all of the subscribing witnesses have died, have left the state, or have become incompetent or unavailable, the instrument may be proved by any person who will state under oath that he or she knows the handwriting of the maker of the instrument and that the signature on the instrument is the maker's.[25] The instrument may also be proved if the person states under oath that he or she knows the handwriting of a subscribing witness and that the signature on the document is that of the subscribing witness.[26] Again, if the subscribing witness is a beneficiary or grantee in the instrument, his or her signature may not be proved.

If the instrument has no subscribing witnesses, it may be proved by any person who will state under oath that he or she knows the handwriting of the maker and that the signature on the instrument is the maker's.[27]

Certificate Forms of Acknowledgment and Proof

Introduction
All notarial acts must include the following components to satisfy legal requirements:

1. The name of the state and county in which the certification occurs
2. The body of the certificate, stating before whom, by whom, and in what manner the signature was acknowledged or proved
3. The date of acknowledgment or proof
4. The signature and seal of the officer who took the acknowledgment or proof[28]
5. The expiration date of the officer's commission

The name of the person whose signature is being acknowledged or proved should be typed or printed in the certificate exactly as it was signed on the document. Some notaries add to their certificates the words "Let the instrument with this certificate be registered" or a similar expression, but this phrase is not required and has no legal significance. The notary's certificate must be written on the document or attached to it in a manner (by glue or staples, for example)

---

24. G.S. 47-12.2.
25. G.S. 47-12.1.
26. *Id.*
27. G.S. 47-13.
28. *See, e.g.,* G.S. 47-38 and -41.01.

making detachment unlikely. When motor vehicle title documents are acknowledged, the acknowledgment must be on the document itself.

Many instruments drafted by the parties or their attorneys have blank certificate forms already attached. Determining whether the certificate has the desired legal effect is the responsibility of the parties and their attorneys; the notary's duty is to ensure that the recitals of the certificate are accurate. Many printed instruments include several blank certificates from which the one suitable to the situation must be selected.

When an instrument is presented without a certificate form, or without one that may be adapted to the circumstances, an applicable form should be made out by either a party to the instrument or an attorney and attached to the instrument. Should questions arise about a certificate's validity or suitability, it is usually better to type a new certificate than to alter materially the face of a printed form.

Various forms for certifying the acknowledgment or proof of the execution of instruments follow. Many sample proof certificates are also available at http://www.secretary.state.nc.us/notary/, Web site of The Notary Public Section of the North Carolina Department of the Secretary of State. This chapter provides an explanation of each form and the blank form, with instructions for its completion. Then an example of a completed form is shown. The language of most of the forms is statutory; however, some forms derive from statutory requirements providing no precise wording. When precise language is required by statute, that statute is cited in a footnote.

Although *substantial* compliance with most of the forms is sufficient for legal validity, the statutory wording should be followed closely, because what may seem an inconsequential variation to the notary can actually be an omission or alteration invalidating the certificate. As will be explained later, the form for the short-form power of attorney must contain the exact wording in the statutes or the register of deeds will not record the instrument. The personal pronouns used in the forms, most of which are masculine and singular, should be altered to fit the individual case.

Instruments executed by individuals

Acknowledgment of instrument signed by one person

When an instrument is executed by a person in his or her individual capacity who personally appears before the notary to acknowledge his or her signature, this is the proper certificate.[29]

---

29. G.S. 47-38.

North Carolina
_____**A**_____ County

I, _____**B**_____, a Notary Public for _____**C**_____ County, North Carolina, do hereby certify that _____**D**_____ personally appeared before me this day and acknowledged the due execution of the foregoing instrument.

Witness my hand and official seal, this the __**E**__ day of _____**F**_____, 20 **G** .

(Official Seal)   _____**H**_____
                                        Notary Public

My commission expires _____**I**_____, 20 __**J**__ .

A. County in which acknowledgment taken.

B. Typed or printed name of notary exactly as it appears in the seal or stamp.

C. County in which notary commissioned.

D. Typed or printed name of person whose acknowledgment is being taken exactly as name appears on the signature line.

E. Date acknowledgment taken.

F. Month acknowledgment taken.

G. Year acknowledgment taken.

H. Notary's signature.

I. Month and date notary's commission expires.

J. Year notary's commission expires.

Example: Slim Beane appeared before John Apple, a Wake County notary, to execute a deed on March 15, 2003. Apple's commission expires April 15, 2007. The acknowledgment was taken in Alexander County.

North Carolina
__**Alexander**_____ County

I, _____**John Apple**_____, a Notary Public for ____**Wake**____ County, North Carolina, do hereby certify that _____**Slim Beane**_____ personally appeared before me this day and acknowledged the due execution of the foregoing instrument.

Witness my hand and official seal, this the __**15th**__ day of ____**March**____, 20 **03** .

(Official Seal)   _John Apple_
                                        Notary Public

My commission expires _____**April 15**_____, 20 **07** .

Acknowledgment of instrument signed by two or more persons

When an instrument is executed by two or more persons and their acknowledgments are taken before different notaries at different times, each notary must execute a certificate for the individual whose acknowledgment is being taken, as indicated previously. If their acknowledgments are taken before the same notary at the same time, the proper form is shown below.[30]

North Carolina

_____**A**_____ County

I, _____**B**_____, a Notary Public for _____**C**_____ County, North Carolina, do hereby certify that _____**D**_____ and_____**E**_____ personally appeared before me this day and acknowledged the due execution of the foregoing instrument.

Witness my hand and official seal, this the ____**F**____ day of _____**G**_____, 20 __**H**__.

    (Official Seal)   _____**I**_____

                                      Notary Public

My commission expires _____**J**_____, 20 __**K**__.

A. County in which acknowledgment taken.	E. See "D".
B. Typed or printed name of notary exactly as it appears in the seal or stamp.	F. Date acknowledgment taken.
	G. Month acknowledgment taken.
C. County in which notary commissioned.	H. Year acknowledgment taken.
D. Typed or printed name of person whose acknowledgment is being taken exactly as name appears on the signature line.	I. Notary's signature.
	J. Month and date notary's commission expires.
	K. Year notary's commission expires.

Example: Ruby Jewell and Opal Jewell appeared before Melville Hawthorne, an Anson County notary, to execute a deed on July 6, 2003. Hawthorne's commission expires December 1, 2004. The acknowledgments were taken in Wadesboro.

North Carolina

_____**Anson**_____ County

I, _____**Melville Hawthorn**_____, a Notary Public for _____**Anson**_____ County, North Carolina, do hereby certify that _____**Ruby Jewell**_____ and_____**Opal Jewell**_____ personally appeared before me this day and acknowledged the due execution of the foregoing instrument.

Witness my hand and official seal, this the ____**6th**____ day of _____**July**_____, 20 __**03**__.

    (Official Seal)   *Melville Hawthorne*

                                      Notary Public

My commission expires _____**December 1**_____, 20 __**04**__.

---

30. *See* G.S. 47-40.

Acknowledgment by attorney in fact

The statutes require that an acknowledgment by an attorney in fact under a power of attorney be given under oath. Since no oath is specified, the oath found under "Proof of Execution, Procedure" on page 24 will satisfy the requirement. When an instrument is executed for another person by an attorney in fact under a power of attorney, the acknowledgment should be certified as follows:[31]

North Carolina

_____**A**_____ County

I, _____**B**_____, a Notary Public for _____**C**_____County, North Carolina, do hereby certify that _____**D**_____, attorney in fact for _____**E**_____, personally appeared before me this day, and being by me duly sworn, says that he executed the foregoing and annexed instrument for and in behalf of the said _____**F**_____, and that his authority to execute and acknowledge said instrument is contained in an instrument duly executed, acknowledged, and recorded in the office of _____**G**_____ in the County of _____**H**_____, State of _____**I**_____, on the ___**J**___ day of ___**K**___, 20 _**L**_, and that this instrument was executed under and by virtue of the authority given by said instrument granting him power of attorney.

I do further certify that the said _____**M**_____ acknowledged the due execution of the foregoing and annexed instrument for the purposes therein expressed for and in behalf of the said _____**N**_____.

Witness my hand and official seal, this the ___**O**___ day of _____**P**_____, 20 _**Q**_.

(Official Seal)   _____**R**_____
                                           Notary Public

My commission expires _____**S**_____, 20 _**T**_.

A. County in which acknowledgment taken.

B. Typed or printed name of notary exactly as it appears in the seal or stamp.

C. County in which notary commissioned.

D. Typed or printed name of attorney in fact executing document.

E. Typed or printed name of person for whom attorney in fact is acting.

F. See "E."

G. Recording office in which power of attorney filed.

H. County in which power of attorney filed.

I. State in which power of attorney filed.

J. Date power of attorney filed.

K. Month power of attorney filed.

L. Year power of attorney filed.

M. See "D."

N. See "E."

O. Date acknowledgment taken.

P. Month acknowledgment taken.

Q. Year acknowledgment taken.

R. Notary's signature.

S. Month and date notary's commission expires.

T. Year notary's commission expires.

---

31. G.S. 47-43.

Example: May Ishmael gave her power of attorney to George Ishmael, and the instrument was recorded in the Dare County registry on June 30, 2003. On August 14, 2003, George executed a deed on behalf of May and acknowledged the execution before Sherlock Watson, a Hyde County notary. Watson's commission expires November 28, 2007. The acknowledgment was taken in Swan Quarter.

North Carolina

_____**Hyde**_____ County

I, _____**Sherlock Watson**_____, a Notary Public for _____**Hyde**_____County, North Carolina, do hereby certify that _____**George Ishmael**_____, attorney in fact for _____**May Ishmael**_____, personally appeared before me this day, and being by me duly sworn, says that he executed the foregoing and annexed instrument for and in behalf of the said __**May Ishmael**__, and that his authority to execute and acknowledge said instrument is contained in an instrument duly executed, acknowledged, and recorded in the office of **Register of Deeds** in the County of _____**Dare**_____, State of **North Carolina**, on the **30th** day of __**June**__, 20**03**, and that this instrument was executed under and by virtue of the authority given by said instrument granting him power of attorney.

I do further certify that the said __**George Ishmael**__ acknowledged the due execution of the foregoing and annexed instrument for the purposes therein expressed for and in behalf of the said __**May Ishmael**__.

Witness my hand and official seal, this the __**14th**__ day of _____**August**_____, 20**03**.

(Official Seal)   *Sherlock Watson*
                                    Notary Public

My commission expires _____**November 28**_____, 20**07**.

Proof by subscribing witness

As described earlier, an instrument that has one or more subscribing witnesses may be proved by the sworn testimony of one of these witnesses. The form of the certificate is shown here.[32]

North Carolina

_____**A**_____ County

I, _____**B**_____, a Notary Public of _____**C**_____ County,

_____**D**_____, certify that _____**E**_____ personally appeared before me this day, and being duly sworn, stated that in his presence _____**F**_____ (signed) (acknowledged the execution of) the foregoing instrument.

Witness my hand and official seal, this the ___**G**___ day of _____**H**_____, 20 __**I**__.

(Official Seal)   _____**J**_____
                                                         Notary Public

My commission expires _____**K**_____, 20 __**L**__.

A. County in which proof taken.	F. Typed or printed name of person who executed instrument being proved exactly as name appears on the signature line.
B. Typed or printed name of notary exactly as it appears in the seal or stamp.	
C. County in which notary commissioned.	G. Date acknowledgment taken.
D. State in which notary commissioned.	H. Month acknowledgment taken.
E. Typed or printed name of witness proving document exactly as name appears from his or her signature as a subscribing witness to the instrument.	I. Year acknowledgment taken.
	J. Notary's signature.
	K. Month and date notary's commission expires.
	L. Year notary's commission expires.

Example: Narley Pratt executed a deed to his land in Madison County. Shepard Ladd was a subscribing witness to Pratt's execution of the deed. On November 11, 2003, Ladd appeared before Bonnie Doone, a Buncombe County notary, to prove the execution of the instrument. Doone's commission expires July 1, 2007. The proof was taken in Asheville.

North Carolina

_____**Buncombe**_____ County

I, _____**Bonnie Doone**_____, a Notary Public of _____**Buncombe**_____ County,

_____**North Carolina**_____, certify that _____**Shepard Ladd**_____ personally appeared before me this day, and being duly sworn, stated that in his presence _____**Narley Pratt**_____ (signed) (acknowledged the execution of) the foregoing instrument.

Witness my hand and official seal, this the __**11th**__ day of _____**November**_____, 20 __**03**__.

(Official Seal)   *Bonnie Doone*
                                                         Notary Public

My commission expires _____**July 1**_____, 20 __**07**__.

---

32. G.S. 47-43.2.

Proof by other person: signature of person who executed

When there are no subscribing witnesses to an instrument or they are unavailable, the execution of the instrument may be proved by a person who can recognize the handwriting of either the person who executed the instrument[33] or a subscribing witness.[34] The proper forms for these methods of proof are here and on pages 33–34:

North Carolina
_____**A**_____ County

I, _____**B**_____, a Notary Public of _____**C**_____ County,
_____**D**_____, certify that _____**E**_____ personally appeared
before me this day, and being duly sworn, stated that he knows the handwriting of
_____**F**_____ and that the signature to the foregoing instrument is the signature
of _____**G**_____.

Witness my hand and official seal, this the ___**H**___ day of _____**I**_____, 20 **J**__.

(Official Seal)   _____**K**_____
                                        Notary Public

My commission expires _____**L**_____, 20 **M**__.

A. County in which proof taken.
B. Typed or printed name of notary exactly as it appears in the seal or stamp.
C. County in which notary commissioned.
D. State in which notary commissioned.
E. Typed or printed name of person proving signature.
F. Typed or printed name of person who executed instrument being proved exactly as name appears on the signature line.
G. See "F."
H. Date proof taken.
I. Month proof taken.
J. Year proof taken.
K. Notary's signature.
L. Month and date notary's commission expires.
M. Year notary's commission expires.

Example: Knox Calvin executed a deed to his property in Franklin County. On February 3, 2003, Francis Xavier appeared before Stormy Skye, a Franklin County notary, to prove Calvin's signature on the instrument. Skye's commission expires October 13, 2007. The proof was taken in Louisburg.

---

33. G.S. 47-43.3.
34. G.S. 47-43.4.

North Carolina

_____**Franklin**_____ County

I, _____**Stormy Skye**_____, a Notary Public of __**Franklin**__ County,
_____**North Carolina**_____, certify that __**Francis Xavier**__ personally appeared
before me this day, and being duly sworn, stated that he knows the handwriting of
_____**Knox Calvin**_____ and that the signature to the foregoing instrument is the signature
of __**Knox Calvin**__.

Witness my hand and official seal, this the __**3rd**__ day of __**February**__, 20 **03**.

(Official Seal)   _Stormy Skye_
                                    Notary Public

My commission expires _____**October 13**_____, 20 **07**.

Proof by other person: signature of subscribing witness

North Carolina

_____**A**_____ County

I, _____**B**_____, a Notary Public of _____**C**_____ County,
_____**D**_____, certify that _____**E**_____ personally appeared
before me this day, and being duly sworn, stated that he knows the handwriting of
_____**F**_____, and that the signature of _____**G**_____ as a subscrib-
ing witness to the foregoing instrument is the signature of _____**H**_____.

Witness my hand and official seal, this the __**I**__ day of _____**J**_____, 20 **K**.

(Official Seal)   _____**L**_____
                                    Notary Public

My commission expires _____**M**_____, 20 **N**.

A. County in which proof taken.
B. Typed or printed name of notary exactly as it appears in the seal or stamp.
C. County in which notary commissioned.
D. State in which notary commissioned.
E. Typed or printed name of person proving signature of subscribing witness.
F. Typed or printed name of subscribing witness exactly as name appears on the signature line.
G. See "F".
H. See "F."
I. Date proof taken.
J. Month proof taken.
K. Year proof taken.
L. Notary's signature.
M. Month and date notary's commission expires.
N. Year notary's commission expires.

Example: John Little executed a will in Columbus County, with Ernest Mann as a subscribing witness. On March 30, 2003, Earl Grey appeared before Ashley Lee Cavanaugh, a Columbus County notary, to prove Mann's signature as a subscribing witness. Cavanaugh's commission expires March 31, 2007. The proof was taken in Whiteville.

North Carolina
_____**Columbus**_____ County

I, __**Ashley Lee Cavanaugh**__, a Notary Public of __**Columbus**__ County, _____**North Carolina**_____, certify that _____**Earl Grey**_____ personally appeared before me this day, and being duly sworn, stated that he knows the handwriting of _____**Ernest Mann**_____, and that the signature of __**Ernest Mann**__ as a subscribing witness to the foregoing instrument is the signature of __**Ernest Mann**__.
Witness my hand and official seal, this the __**30th**__ day of _____**March**_____, 20__**03**__.

(Official Seal)   *Ashley Lee Cavanaugh*
                                         Notary Public

My commission expires _____**March 31**_____, 20 __**07**__.

Instruments executed by trustees

A trust is an arrangement in which property, either real or personal, is managed by a trustee for the benefit of another person, the beneficiary. Instruments executed by a person as trustee are his or her own acts and must be acknowledged or proved in the manner set forth in the preceding sections for individuals. A trustee should sign an instrument in a manner that indicates the capacity in which he or she acts, and the certificate of acknowledgment or proof should indicate that he or she has signed as trustee.[35]

Example of execution by trustee

Joe Colorado
Joe Colorado
Trustee for Roger Hill

The text of the acknowledgment should read:

I, _____, a Notary Public for _____ County,
North Carolina, do hearby certify that **Joe Colorado, Trustee for Roger Hill**, personally
appeared before me this day and acknowledged the due execution of the foregoing instrument.

---

35. *See* Hayes v. Ferguson, 206 N.C. 414, 174 S.E. 121 (1934).

Instruments executed by partnerships

A partnership is an unincorporated association of two or more persons formed to do business for profit.[36] Within certain limits, the business-related acts of a partner will bind the other partners.[37] Real property belonging to a partnership must be conveyed in the name of the partnership, but ordinarily any one of the partners may execute the conveyance in the partnership name.[38] The forms for acknowledgment or proof of instruments executed by individuals may be used for certificates of individual partners, and the certificates should indicate the capacity in which the individual partner signs.

Example of execution by partner

John R. Tweedledum

T & T Hats, A Partnership,
by John R. Tweedledum, a partner

The text of the acknowledgment should read:

I, _____, a Notary Public for _____ County,
North Carolina, do hearby certify that **John R. Tweedledum,** a partner in **T&T Hats**,
                                       (Name of partner)   (Name of partnership)
personally appeared before me this day and acknowledged the due execution of the foregoing
instrument on behalf of the parnership.

Instruments executed by persons doing business under assumed names

Persons doing business under assumed names—other than partnership or corporation names—should sign documents concerning their businesses in a manner indicating the capacity in which they act, and the certificate of acknowledgment or proof should indicate this capacity.

Example of execution under an assumed name

Zoot Hawkins

Zoot Hawkins/Doing business as
Hot Shot Records

---

36. G.S. 59-36.
37. G.S. 59-39.
38. G.S. 59-38(c) and -39.

The text of the acknowledgment should read:

> I, _____, a Notary Public for _____ County,
> North Carolina, do hearby certify that ___**Zoot Hawkins/DBA Hot Shot Records**___
> personally appeared before me this day and acknowledged the due execution of the foregoing
> instrument.

Instruments executed by limited liability companies

A limited liability company is a form of business organization created pursuant to G.S. Chapter 57C that shares some of the characteristics of a partnership and some of a corporation. Limited liability company instruments are usually executed by one of the company's managers, and they are not required to be attested.

Example of execution by a limited liability company

> _Verdant Field_(SEAL)
>
> Green Hills, L.L.C.
> By: **Verdant Field, Manager**
> (Name and title of manager)

The text of the acknowledgment should read:

> I, _____, a Notary Public for _____ County,
> North Carolina, do hearby certify **Verdant Field, Manager of Green Hills, L.L.C.** , a
>   (Name of manager, title, name of L.L.C.)
> limited liability company, personally appeared before me this day and acknowledged the due
> execution of the foregoing instrument on behalf of the company.

Instruments executed by religious bodies or denominations

The trustees of any religious body may mortgage or sell land owned by the religious group when the group directs them to do so.[39] The trustees should sign the instrument in a manner indicating the capacity in which they act, and the certificate of acknowledgment or proof should indicate this capacity. The form of the certificate is the one used for individuals.

Example of execution by church trustees

> _John MacDuff, Hugh MacBeth, Hamish Malcolm_
> John MacDuff, Hugh MacBeth, Hamish Malcolm
> Trustees for **Church of the Rock**

---

39. G.S. 61-4.

The text of the acknowledgment should read:

> I, _____, a Notary Public for _____ County,
> North Carolina, do hearby certify that **John MacDuff, Hugh Macbeth, Hamish Malcolm**,
> Trustees for_____**Church of the Rock**_____, personally appeared before me this
> day and acknowledged the due execution of the foregoing instrument.

In addition, ecclesiastical officers, such as ministers or bishops, designated by a religious group to administer its affairs may convey the property of that group.[40] The execution by such an officer is acknowledged or proved in the same manner as an execution by an individual, and the certificate of acknowledgment should indicate the capacity in which the ecclesiastical officer signed.

Example of execution by an ecclesiastical officer

> *Joseph Victor McCarroll*
>
> Joseph Victor McCarroll, Bishop of the Carolinas

The text of the acknowledgment should read:

> I, _____, a Notary Public for _____ County,
> North Carolina, do hearby certify that **Joseph Victor McCarroll, Bishop of the Carolinas,**
> personally appeared before me this day and acknowledged the due execution of the foregoing
> instrument.

Instruments executed by voluntary associations

A voluntary association of persons organized for charitable, fraternal, religious, social, or patriotic purposes may hold real property either through trustees or in the association's name.[41] Property held through trustees may be conveyed by an instrument executed by them as trustees and acknowledged or proved in the manner previously described for individuals.[42] The notary adds to his or her certificate the fact that they have executed the instrument as trustees of the named association. When the transaction is authorized by the voluntary association, real estate held in the association's name may be conveyed "by a deed signed by its chairman or president, and its secretary or treasurer, or such officer as is the custodian of its common seal with its official seal affixed, the said conveyance to be proven and probated in the same manner as provided by law for deeds by corporations. . . ."[43]

---

40. G.S. 61-5.
41. G.S. 39-24 and -26.
42. G.S. 39-26.
43. G.S. 39-25.

Forms for proving the execution of corporate conveyances are set out below. In applying the forms to conveyances by voluntary associations, the phrase "voluntary association" should be substituted wherever the word "corporation" appears, and the term "common seal" should replace "corporate seal."

Instruments executed by corporations

The law carefully specifies the methods by which corporate authority may be delegated, exercised, and authenticated,[44] because a corporation is a legal person separate from the individuals who are its officers, directors, and stockholders; it is bound only by the authorized acts of its agents. Adherence to the statutory requirements and forms ensures that corporate instruments are legitimate acts of the corporation rather than unauthorized acts of individuals.

Instruments executed by corporations will usually include the necessary certificate forms. Whenever a notary prepares his or her own certificate of acknowledgment or proof for an instrument executed by a corporation, he or she should select the form in this section that fits the particular circumstances.

G.S. 47-41.01 and -41.02 set out five different forms of acknowledgment that may be used for a corporate deed, deed of trust, or other instrument conveying an interest in real estate. The first form in G.S. 47-41.01 and the third form in G.S. 47-41.02 both certify an instrument that has three essential components: (1) the instrument is executed by one officer of the corporation, (2) the instrument is attested (witnessed) by another officer of the corporation, and (3) the corporate seal is affixed. The second form in G.S. 47-41.01 does not require attestation or a corporate seal.

Instruments conveying security interest in personal property of a corporation

When a contract creates a security interest in the personal property of a corporation, the contract will usually be signed by one of the following corporate officers: the president, a vice-president, the secretary, an assistant secretary, the treasurer, or an assistant treasurer. The statutes do not require that such contracts bear the corporate seal or be attested by another corporate officer.[45] Here is the proper acknowledgment form for these contracts:

---

44. *See, e.g.*, G.S. 47-41.01, 55-8-40, and 55-8-41.
45. *See* G.S. 47-41.02(f).

North Carolina

_____ **A** _____ County

I, _____ **B** _____, a Notary Public for _____ **C** _____ County, North
Carolina, do hereby certify that _____ **D** _____ personally came before me this
day and acknowledged that he is _____ **E** _____ of
_____ **F** _____, and acknowledged, on behalf of
_____ **G** _____, the due execution of the foregoing instrument.

Witness my hand and official seal, this the ___ **H** ___ day of _____ **I** _____, 20 **J** .

(Official Seal) _____ **K** _____
Notary Public

My commission expires _____ **L** _____, 20 **M** .

A. County in which acknowledgment taken.
B. Typed or printed name of notary exactly as it
   appears in the seal or stamp.
C. County in which notary commissioned.
D. Typed or printed name of corporate officer
   executing document exactly as name appears
   on the signature line.
E. Title of corporate officer executing
   instrument.

F. Corporation of which the person who signs
   is an officer.
G. See "F."
H. Date acknowledgment taken.
I. Month acknowledgment taken.
J. Year acknowledgment taken.
K. Notary's signature.
L. Month and date notary's commission expires.
M. Year notary's commission expires.

Example: Timothy Cruise, president of the Juice & Sauce Corporation,
executed a document giving a security interest in the corporation's personal
property to First National Bank. Cruise appeared before Tuesday Morning, a
Duplin County notary, on July 3, 2003, to acknowledge execution of the
instrument. Morning's commission expires July 4, 2007. The acknowledgment was taken in Kenansville.

North Carolina

_____ **Duplin** _____ County

I, __ **Tuesday Morning** __, a Notary Public for _____ **Duplin** _____ County, North
Carolina, do hereby certify that __ **Timothy Cruise** __ personally came before me this
day and acknowledged that he is _____ **President** __ of
__ **Juice & Sauce Corporation** __, and acknowledged, on behalf of
__ **Juice & Sauce Corporation** __, the due execution of the foregoing instrument.

Witness my hand and official seal, this the __ **3rd** __ day of __ **July** __, 20 **03** .

(Official Seal) *Tuesday Morning*
Notary Public

My commission expires _____ **July 4** _____, 20 **07** .

Instruments conveying a corporate interest in real property

Acknowledgment by attesting officer

For this form to be used, the instrument must have been executed by the chairman, chief executive officer, president, vice-president, assistant vice-president, treasurer, or chief financial officer. It must have been attested by the secretary, assistant secretary, trust officer, assistant trust officer, associate trust officer, or—in the case of a bank—the secretary, assistant secretary, cashier, or assistant cashier.[46] The officer signing the instrument must do so in the name of the corporation. Only the attesting officer need appear before the notary to give the acknowledgment.

North Carolina

_____**A**_____ County

I, _____**B**_____, a Notary Public for _____**C**_____ County, North Carolina, certify that _____**D**_____ personally came before me this day and acknowledged that he is _____**E**_____ of _____**F**_____, a corporation, and that by authority duly given and as the act of the corporation the foregoing instrument was signed in its name by its _____**G**_____, sealed with its corporate seal, and attested by himself as its _____**H**_____.

Witness my hand and official seal, this the ___**I**___ day of _____**J**_____, 20 _**K**_.

(Official Seal)   _____**L**_____
                              Notary Public

My commission expires _____**M**_____, 20 **N**.

A. County in which acknowledgment taken.
B. Typed or printed name of notary exactly as it appears in the seal or stamp.
C. County in which notary commissioned.
D. Typed or printed name of officer attesting the instrument's execution exactly as name appears on the signature line of attestation.
E. Title of officer attesting.
F. Corporation.
G. Title of officer signing instrument.
H. See "E."
I. Date acknowledgment taken.
J. Month acknowledgment taken.
K. Year acknowledgment taken.
L. Notary's signature.
M. Month and date notary's commission expires.
N. Year notary's commission expires.

Example: Jenny Longfellow, president of Walden Grits Company, executed a deed to corporate property, and Melissa Thoreau, secretary of the company, attested the execution. On August 11, 2003, Thoreau appeared before Henry Wadsworth, a Macon County notary, to acknowledge the instrument. Wadsworth's commission expires September 15, 2007. The acknowledgment was taken in Greensboro.

---

46. G.S. 47-41.01.

North Carolina
__**Guilford**_____ County

I, __**Henry Wadsworth**_____, a Notary Public for __**Macon**____ County, North Carolina, certify that _____**Melissa Thoreau**_____ personally came before me this day and acknowledged that she is _____**Secretary**_____ of **Walden Grits Company**, a corporation, and that by authority duly given and as the act of the corporation the foregoing instrument was signed in its name by its _____**President**_____, sealed with its corporate seal, and attested by herself as its _____**Secretary**_____.

Witness my hand and official seal, this the __**11th**__ day of __**August**_____, 20 **03**.

(Official Seal)   _~~Henry Wadsworth~~_____
                                 Notary Public

My commission expires _____**September 15**_____, 20 **07**.

Acknowledgment by signing officer

The form set out below is for use when the corporate officer who executed the instrument acknowledges its execution. For this form to be used, the instrument must have been executed by the president, vice-president, presiding member, or trustee of the corporation and attested by its secretary or assistant secretary.[47] The officer acknowledging its execution must be placed under oath.

North Carolina
_____**A**_____ County

This ____**B**____ day of ____**C**____, 20 **D**, personally came before me,
_____**E**_____, Notary Public for _____**F**_____ County, North Carolina, _____**G**_____, who, being by me duly sworn, says that he is _____**H**_____ of the _____**I**_____, a corporation, and that the seal affixed to the foregoing instrument in writing is the corporate seal of said company, and that said writing was signed and sealed by him in behalf of said corporation by its authority duly given. And the said _____**J**_____ acknowledged the said writing to be the act and deed of said corporation.

Witness my hand and official seal, this the __**K**____ day of _____**L**_____, 20 **M**__.

(Official Seal)   _____**N**_____
                                 Notary Public

My commission expires _____**O**_____, 20 **P**__.

A. County in which acknowledgment taken.	H. Title of officer who executed instrument.
B. Date acknowledgment taken.	I. Corporation.
C. Month acknowledgment taken.	J. See "G."
D. Year acknowledgment taken.	K. Date acknowledgment taken.
E. Typed or printed name of notary exactly as it appears in the seal or stamp.	L. Month acknowledgment taken.
	M. Year acknowledgment taken.
F. County in which notary commissioned.	N. Notary's signature.
G. Typed or printed name of officer who executed instrument exactly as name appears on the signature line.	O. Month and date notary's commission expires.
	P. Year notary's commission expires.

---

47. G.S. 47-41.02.

Example: Sara Lee Baker, president of New River Steel Company, executed a deed to corporate property. Her signature was attested by the corporate secretary, Bonnie Amy Sink. Baker acknowledged execution of the instrument on November 12, 2003, before Homer Scrub, an Ashe County notary. Scrub's commission expires December 13, 2007. The acknowledgment was taken in Jefferson.

North Carolina

_____**Ashe**_____ County

This ___**12th**___ day of **November** , 20 **03** , personally came before me,
_____**Homer Scrub**_____ , Notary Public for _____**Ashe**_____ County, North Carolina, _____**Sara Lee Baker**_____ , who, being by me duly sworn, says that she is _____**President**_____ of the ___**New River Steel Company**___ , a corporation, and that the seal affixed to the foregoing instrument in writing is the corporate seal of said company, and that said writing was signed and sealed by her in behalf of said corporation by its authority duly given. And the said ___**Sara Lee Baker**___ acknowledged the said writing to be the act and deed of said corporation.

Witness my hand and official seal, this the ___**12th**___ day of ___**November**___ , 20 **03** .

(Official Seal)   *Homer Scrub*
_____
                       Notary Public

My commission expires _____**December 13**_____ , 20 **07** .

Acknowledgment without attestation

The form set out below is a form of corporate acknowledgment authorized by G.S. 47-41.01(c). It does not require attestation or the presence of a corporate seal.

North Carolina

_____**A**_____ County

I, _____**B**_____, a Notary Public for _____**C**_____ County, North Carolina, certify that _____**D**_____ personally came before me this day and acknowledged that he (or she) is _____**E**_____ of _____**F**_____, a corporation, and that he (or she), as _____**G**_____, being authorized to do so, executed the foregoing on behalf of the corporation.

Witness my hand and official seal, this the **H** day of _____**I**_____, 20 **J**.

    (Official Seal)   _____**K**_____

                                Notary Public

My commission expires __**L**__, _____**M**_____, 20 **N**.

A. County in which acknowledgment taken.

B. Typed or printed name of notary exactly as it appears in the seal or stamp.

C. County in which notary commissioned.

D. Name of person who signed exactly as typed or printed on the signature line.

E. Title of person who signed exactly as typed or printed on the signature line.

F. Corporation on behalf of which the officer signed.

G. See "E."

H. Date acknowledgment taken.

I. Month acknowledgment taken.

J. Year acknowledgment taken.

K. Notary's signature.

L. Month notary's commission expires.

M. Date notary's commission expires.

N. Year notary's commission expires.

Example: Willie Westin, vice-president of the High Lonesome Corporation, executed a deed to corporate property. Westin acknowledged the execution of the deed on May 5, 2004, before Hannah Harley, a Stokes County notary. Harley's commission expires July 10, 2006. The acknowledgment was taken in Dobson.

North Carolina

_____**Surry**_____ County

I, __**Hannah Harley**__, a Notary Public for _____**Stokes**_____ County, North Carolina, certify that _____**Willie Westin**_____ personally came before me this day and acknowledged that he (or she) is __**Vice-President**__ of __**High Lonesome Corp.**__, a corporation, and that he (or she), as __**Vice-President**__, being authorized to do so, executed the foregoing on behalf of the corporation.

Witness my hand and official seal, this the **5th** day of __**May**__, 20**04**.

    (Official Seal)   *Hannah Harley*

                             Notary Public

My commission expires _____**July 10**_____, 20 **06**.

Short-Form Powers of Attorney

G.S. 32A-1 sets out a statutory form for a power of attorney, called a "Short Form of General Power of Attorney." Any power of attorney that follows this form will recite in its heading that it is granting powers as defined in Chapter 32A. A power of attorney executed pursuant to this statute must be acknowledged with the certificate below. The exact language of this certificate is required by statute and must be followed word for word.[48] Note that the person acknowledging the execution must be placed under oath. Any deviation from the statutory language of the certificate will cause the register of deeds to reject the power of attorney when it is offered for registration.

Example of short-form power of attorney

State of _____ **A** _____
County of _____ **B** _____

On this ___ **C** ___ day of _____ **D** ___, 20 **E** , personally appeared before me, the said named _____ **F** _____, to me known and known to me to be the person described in and who executed the foregoing instrument and he (or she) acknowledged that he (or she) executed the same and being duly sworn by me, made oath that the statements in the foregoing instrument are true.

My commission expires _____ **G** _____, 20 **H** .

(Official Seal)   _____ **I** _____
                                              Notary Public
                                   [_____ **J** _____]

A. State in which acknowledgment taken.
B. County in which acknowledgment taken.
C. Date acknowledgment taken.
D. Month acknowledgment taken.
E. Year acknowledgment taken.
F. Typed or printed name of person executing the power of attorney exactly as this name appears on the signature line.

G. Month and date notary's commission expires.
H. Year notary's commission expires.
I. Notary's signature.
J. Because no space is in the text of the acknowledgment for the notary's typed or printed name, it is a good idea to add it in brackets just below the signature line. It should appear exactly as in the notary's seal or stamp.

Example: George Brown executed a short-form power of attorney to his wife, Grace. He appeared before Natalie Farrantino, a Tyrrell County notary, on August 14, 2003, to acknowledge execution of the instrument. Farrantino's commission expires September 3, 2006. The acknowledgment was taken in Columbia.

---

48. *See* G.S. 32A-1.

State of **North Carolina**

County of _____**Tyrrell**_____

On this **14th** day of ____**August**____ , 20 **03** , personally appeared before me, the said named _____**George Brown**_____ , to me known and known to me to be the person described in and who executed the foregoing instrument and <u>he</u> (~~or she~~) acknowledged that <u>he</u> (~~or she~~) executed the same and being duly sworn by me, made oath that the statements in the foregoing instrument are true.

My commission expires _____**September 3**_____ , 20 **06** .

      (Official Seal)   *Natalie Farrantino*

                                     Notary Public

                     [**Natalie Farrantino**   ]

Wills

Ordinary attested wills

An ordinary attested will is attested by two witnesses, and its execution need not be acknowledged or proved before a notary.[49] Such a will is probated by having the witnesses to the will appear before the clerk of superior court and answer certain questions.[50]

Self-proved wills

Example of executing self-proved will

Most wills executed today are self-proved; that is, they are executed in accordance with certain statutory requirements, and the witnesses therefore need not appear before the clerk of superior court to prove the will, the proof being contained in the document itself. For a will to be self-proved, a notary or other officer authorized to administer oaths is required. A will can be made self-proving in two ways, the first of which is when it is executed and attested. For this way, the following certificates are used.[51] Note that the testator (person making the will) and the witnesses must be placed under oath.

---

49. *See* G.S. 31-3.3.
50. *See* G.S. 31-18.1.
51. G.S. 31-11.6(a).

I, _____**A**_____, the testator, sign my name to this instrument this ___**B**___ day of
____**C**____, 20_**D**_, and being first duly sworn, do hereby declare to the undersigned
authority that I sign and execute this instrument as my last will and that I sign it willingly (or
willingly direct another to sign for me), that I execute it as my free and voluntary act for the
purposes therein expressed, and that I am eighteen years of age or older, of sound mind, and
under no constraint or undue influence.

_____**E**_____
Testator

We, _____**F**_____, _____**G**_____, the witnesses, sign our names to this
instrument, being first duly sworn, and do hereby declare to the undersigned authority that the
testator signs and executes this instrument as his last will and that he signs it willingly (or willingly directs another to sign for him), and that each of us, in the presence and hearing of the
testator, hereby signs this will as witness to the testator's signing, and to the best of our
knowledge the testator is eighteen years of age or older, of sound mind, and under no constraint
or undue influence.

_____**H**_____
Witness

_____**I**_____
Witness

The State of _____**J**_____
County of _____**K**_____

Subscribed, sworn to and acknowledged before me by _____**L**_____, the testator, and
subscribed and sworn to before me by _____**M**_____ and _____**N**_____, witnesses, this _**O**_ day of _____**P**_____, 20_**Q**_.

(Official seal or stamp)   _____**R**_____
Notary Public

commission expires _____**S**_____, 20 _**T**_.

A. Typed or printed name of person executing will.
B. Date will is executed.
C. Month will is executed.
D. Year will is executed.
E. Signature of person executing will.
F. Typed or printed name of first witness to will.
G. Typed or printed name of second witness to will.
H. Signature of first witness to will.
I. Signature of second witness to will.
J. State in which acknowledgment taken.

K. County in which acknowledgment taken.
L. See "A."
M. See "F."
N. See "G."
O. Date acknowledgment taken. This date and the following dates should agree with the dates of the execution of the will.
P. Month acknowledgment taken.
Q. Year acknowledgment taken.
R. Notary's signature.
S. Month and date notary's commission expires.
T. Year notary's commission expires.

Example: On February 14, 2004, Roberto Cassini executed his will, with Halston Dior and Polo Dior as witnesses. The acknowledgments to make the will self-proving were taken before a Forsyth County notary, Jules Tiffany. Tiffany's commission expires April 15, 2006. The will was executed and acknowledged in Rural Hall.

I, **Roberto Cassini**_____, the testator, sign my name to this instrument this **14th**__ day of __**Februrary**__, 20_**04**__, and being first duly sworn, do hereby declare to the undersigned authority that I sign and execute this instrument as my last will and that I sign it willingly (or willingly direct another to sign for me), that I execute it as my free and voluntary act for the purposes therein expressed, and that I am eighteen years of age or older, of sound mind, and under no constraint or undue influence.

Roberto Cassini

Testator

We, _____**Halston Dior**_____, _____**Polo Dior**_____, the witnesses, sign our names to this instrument, being first duly sworn, and do hereby declare to the undersigned authority that the testator signs and executes this instrument as his last will and that he signs it willingly (or willingly directs another to sign for him), and that each of us, in the presence and hearing of the testator, hereby signs this will as witness to the testator's signing, and to the best of our knowledge the testator is eighteen years of age or older, of sound mind, and under no constraint or undue influence.

Halston Dior

Witness

Polo Dior

Witness

The State of **North Carolina**____
County of ___**Forsyth**_____

Subscribed, sworn to and acknowledged before me by __**Roberto Cassini**____, the testator, and subscribed and sworn to before me by ____**Halston Dior**____ and _____**Polo Dior**_____, witnesses, this **14th** day of **February**____, 20**04**__.

(Official seal or stamp) _____*Jules Tiffany*_____

Jules Tiffany

Notary Public

My commission expires _____**April 15**_____, 20 **06**__.

Example of certification of will already executed and attested

The second way that a will may be made self-proving is for the testator and witnesses of an already executed and attested will to come before a notary or other officer authorized to administer oaths and make the required acknowledgments using the following certificate.[52] Note that the notary must place the parties under oath.

STATE OF NORTH CAROLINA
COUNTY/CITY OF _____**A**_____

Before me, the undersigned authority, on this day personally appeared
_____**B**_____, _____**C**_____, and
_____**D**_____, known to me to be the testator and the witnesses, respectively, whose names are signed to the attached or foregoing instrument, and all of these persons being by me first duly sworn. The testator declared to me and to the witnesses in my presence: that said instrument is his last will; that he had willingly signed or directed another to sign the same for him, and executed it in the presence of said witnesses as his free and voluntary act for the purposes therein expressed; or that the testator signified that the instrument was his instrument by acknowledging to them his signature previously affixed thereto.

The said witnesses stated before me that the foregoing will was executed and acknowledged by the testator as his last will in the presence of said witnesses who, in his presence and at his request, subscribed their names thereto as attesting witnesses and that the testator, at the time of the execution of said will, was over the age of 18 years and of sound and disposing mind and memory.

_____**E**_____
Testator

_____**F**_____
Witness

_____**G**_____
Witness

Subscribed, sworn to and acknowledged before me by _____**H**_____, the testator, and subscribed and sworn to before me by _____**I**_____ and _____**J**_____, witnesses, the __**K**__ day of _____**L**_____, 20_**M**_.

(Official Seal)   _____**N**_____
                                    Notary Public
My commission expires _____**O**_____, 20_**P**_.

A. County or city in which acknowledgment taken.	I. See "C."
B. Typed or printed name of person who executed will.	J. See "D."
C. Typed or printed name of first witness to will.	K. Date acknowledgment taken.
D. Typed or printed name of second witness to will.	L. Month acknowledgment taken.
E. Signature of person who executed will.	M. Year acknowledgment taken.
F. Signature of first witness to will.	N. Notary's signature.
G. Signature of second witness to will.	O. Month and date notary's commission expires.
H. See "B."	P. Year notary's commission expires.

---

52. G.S. 31-11.6(b).

Example: On March 3, 1991, Julia Beard executed her will, with James Claiborne and Pierre Lee as witnesses. She later decided to convert her will to a self-proving one, and on July 1, 2003, Beard, Claiborne, and Lee appeared before Judith Fisher, a Durham County notary, to make the required acknowledgments. Fisher's commission expires July 2, 2007. The acknowledgments were taken in Durham.

STATE OF NORTH CAROLINA
COUNTY/CITY OF **Durham**

Before me, the undersigned authority, on this day personally appeared **Julia Beard**, **James Claiborne**, and **Pierre Lee**, known to me to be the testator and the witnesses, respectively, whose names are signed to the attached or foregoing instrument, and all of these persons being by me first duly sworn. The testator declared to me and to the witnesses in my presence: that said instrument is her last will; that she had willingly signed or directed another to sign the same for her, and executed it in the presence of said witnesses as her free and voluntary act for the purposes therein expressed; or that the testator signified that the instrument was her instrument by acknowledging to them her signature previously affixed thereto.

The said witnesses stated before me that the foregoing will was executed and acknowledged by the testator as her last will in the presence of said witnesses who, in her presence and at her request, subscribed their names thereto as attesting witnesses and that the testator, at the time of the execution of said will, was over the age of 18 years and of sound and disposing mind and memory.

Julia Beard
Testator

James Claiborne
Witness

Pierre Lee
Witness

Subscribed, sworn to and acknowledged before me by **Julia Beard**, the testator, and subscribed and sworn to before me by **James Claiborne** and **Pierre Lee**, witnesses, the **1st** day of **July**, 20 **03**.

(Official Seal)   *Judith Fisher*
Notary Public

My commission expires **July 2**, 20 **07**.

Living wills

The legislature has provided a means by which a person may state in writing his or her wish that in the event of a terminal or incurable illness extraordinary efforts not be used to prolong his or her life. The document for this is a "Declaration of a Desire for a Natural Death," popularly called a living will. The declaration must be certified, and a notary is one of the officers who may certify it. Note that both the declarant and the witnesses must be placed under oath.[53]

Example of declaration of a desire for a natural death

North Carolina
County of _____**A**_____

CERTIFICATE

I, _____**B**_____, a Notary Public for _____**C**_____ County, North Carolina, hereby certify that _____**D**_____, the declarant, appeared before me and swore to me and to the witnesses in my presence that this instrument is his Declaration Of A Desire For A Natural Death, and that he had willingly and voluntarily made and executed it as his free act and deed for the purposes expressed in it.

I further certify that _____**E**_____ and _____**F**_____, witnesses, appeared before me and swore that they witnessed _____**G**_____, declarant, sign the attached declaration, believing him to be of sound mind; and also swore that at the time they witnessed the declaration (i) they were not related within the third degree to the declarant or to the declarant's spouse, and (ii) they did not know or have a reasonable expectation that they would be entitled to any portion of the estate of the declarant upon the declarant's death under any will of the declarant or codicil thereto then existing or under the Intestate Succession Act as it provides at that time, and (iii) they were not a physician attending the declarant or an employee of an attending physician or an employee of a health facility in which the declarant was a patient or an employee of a nursing home or any group-care home in which the declarant resided, and (iv) they did not have a claim against the declarant. I further certify that I am satisfied as to the genuineness and due execution of the declaration.

This the __**H**__ day of _____**I**_____, 20__**J**__.

(Official Seal) _____**K**_____

Notary Public

for the County of _____**L**_____

My commission expires _____**M**_____, 20__**N**__.

A. County in which acknowledgment taken.	H. Date certification made.
B. Typed or printed name of notary.	I. Month certification made.
C. County in which notary commissioned.	J. Year certification made.
D. Typed or printed name of person signing declaration.	K. Notary's signature.
E. Typed or printed name of first witness.	L. See "C."
F. Typed or printed name of second witness.	M. Month and date notary's commission expires.
G. See "D."	N. Year notary's commission expires.

53. G.S. 90-321.

Example: On March 5, 2004, John Hondo signed a Declaration of a Desire for a Natural Death in the presence of Jack Meany and Matt Irons, witnesses. The certification was made before a Watauga County notary, Kitty Kelly. Kelly's commission expires April 15, 2007. The certificate was made in Boone.

North Carolina
County of **Watauga**

CERTIFICATE

I, **Kitty Kelly** , a Notary Public for **Watauga** County, North Carolina, hereby certify that **John Hondo** , the declarant, appeared before me and swore to me and to the witnesses in my presence that this instrument is his Declaration Of A Desire For A Natural Death, and that he had willingly and voluntarily made and executed it as his free act and deed for the purposes expressed in it.

I further certify that **Jack Meany** and **Matt Irons** , witnesses, appeared before me and swore that they witnessed **John Hondo** , declarant, sign the attached declaration, believing him to be of sound mind; and also swore that at the time they witnessed the declaration (i) they were not related within the third degree to the declarant or to the declarant's spouse, and (ii) they did not know or have a reasonable expectation that they would be entitled to any portion of the estate of the declarant upon the declarant's death under any will of the declarant or codicil thereto then existing or under the Intestate Succession Act as it provides at that time, and (iii) they were not a physician attending the declarant or an employee of an attending physician or an employee of a health facility in which the declarant was a patient or an employee of a nursing home or any group-care home in which the declarant resided, and (iv) they did not have a claim against the declarant. I further certify that I am satisfied as to the genuineness and due execution of the declaration.

This the **5th** day of **March** , 20 **04** .

(Official Seal)   _Kitty Kelly_
                                          Notary Public
              for the County of **Watauga**

My commission expires **April 15** , 20 **07** .

Health Care Powers of Attorney

There is a statutory form by which a person may designate an attorney in fact to deal with certain health care issues, such as the use of extraordinary measures in the event of a terminal illness, organ donations, and disposition of the body. The form calls for the power of attorney to be witnessed by two witnesses. Both the declarant and the witnesses must be sworn.[54]

---

54. G.S. 32A-25.

Example of health care power of attorney

STATE OF NORTH CAROLINA
COUNTY OF_____**A**_____

CERTIFICATE

I, _____**B**_____, a Notary Public for _____**C**_____ County, North Carolina, hereby certify that _____**D**_____ appeared before me and swore to me and to the witnesses in my presence that this instrument is a health care power of attorney, and that he/she willingly and voluntarily made and executed it as his/her free act and deed for the purposes expressed in it.

I further certify that _____**E**_____ and _____**F**_____, witnesses, appeared before me and swore that they witnessed _____**G**_____ sign the attached health care power of attorney, believing him/her to be of sound mind; and also swore that at the time they witnessed the signing (i) they were not related within the third degree to him/her or his/her spouse, and (ii) they did not know nor have a reasonable expectation that they would be entitled to any portion of his/her estate upon his/her death under any will or codicil thereto then existing or under the Intestate Succession Act as it provided at that time, and (iii) they were not a physician attending him/her, nor an employee of an attending physician, nor an employee of a health facility in which he/she was a patient, nor an employee of a nursing home or any group-care home in which he/she resided, and (iv) they did not have a claim against him/her. I further certify that I am satisfied as to the genuineness and due execution of the instrument.

This the ____**H**____ day of _____**I**_____, 20_**J**__.

(Official Seal)   _____**K**_____
                                        Notary Public
                    for the County of _____**L**_____

My commission expires _____**M**_____, 20_**N**__.

A. County in which power of attorney acknowledged.

B. Typed or printed name of notary.

C. County in which notary commissioned.

D. Typed or printed name of person signing power of attorney.

E. Typed or printed name of first witness.

F. Typed or printed name of second witness.

G. See "D."

H. Date certification made.

I. Month certification made.

J. Year certification made.

K. Notary's signature.

L. See "C."

M. Month and date notary's commission expires.

N. Year notary's commission expires.

Example: On July 6, 2003, Golden Rodd signed a health care power of attorney in the presence of Rose Thorne and Daisy White, witnesses. The certification was made before a Columbus County notary, Red Weed. Weed's commission expires March 22, 2007. The certificate was made in Whiteville.

STATE OF NORTH CAROLINA
COUNTY OF **Columbus**

CERTIFICATE

I, **Red Weed**, a Notary Public for **Columbus** County, North Carolina, hereby certify that **Golden Rodd** appeared before me and swore to me and to the witnesses in my presence that this instrument is a health care power of attorney, and that he willingly and voluntarily made and executed it as his free act and deed for the purposes expressed in it.

I further certify that **Rose Thorne** and **Daisy White**, witnesses, appeared before me and swore that they witnessed **Golden Rodd** sign the attached health care power of attorney, believing him/her to be of sound mind; and also swore that at the time they witnessed the signing (i) they were not related within the third degree to him/her or his/her spouse, and (ii) they did not know nor have a reasonable expectation that they would be entitled to any portion of his/her estate upon his/her death under any will or codicil thereto then existing or under the Intestate Succession Act as it provided at that time, and (iii) they were not a physician attending him/her, nor an employee of an attending physician, nor an employee of a health facility in which he/she was a patient, nor an employee of a nursing home or any group-care home in which he/she resided, and (iv) they did not have a claim against him/her. I further certify that I am satisfied as to the genuineness and due execution of the instrument.

This the **6th** day of **July**, 20**03**.

(Official Seal)   *Red Weed*

Notary Public
for the County of **Columbus**

My commission expires **March 22**, 20**07**.

Motor Vehicle Titles

Notaries frequently certify the execution of applications to transfer the title of a motor vehicle or applications for a new title. Several general principles apply to motor vehicle certifications, no matter which Division of Motor Vehicles (DMV) form is used:

1. Be especially careful not to make any spelling or other errors.
2. If an error is made in the first or middle name because of a misspelling or use of a nickname, do not erase it or white it out; instead, draw one line through the error and then correct it above or to the side of the error. If the error is in the last name, an affidavit is required [see 3, below].
3. Any alteration in the last name makes the assignment void. Affidavits from the seller, buyer, and lienholder are required. A new assignment without alterations is required.
4. Be certain that *all* blanks for buyer's and seller's names and addresses, odometer readings, and similar information are filled in before taking the certification.
5. Administer the oath to the person making the certification. Note that persons making a false statement under oath with regard to motor vehicle title documents are guilty of a Class I felony.[55]
6. Require *full* printed names and signatures, just as they appear on the reverse side of the title. This means that a person's middle name must be included; women should provide their given name, previous surname or middle name, and last name.
7. Do not use titles such as "Mr.," "Mrs.," "Ms.," "Dr.," and so forth.
8. If the person whose certification is being taken has no middle name, indicate this fact by inserting the letters "NMN" in the place for a middle name.

If the DMV registration form contains a jurat, "sworn to and subscribed before me," then the notary must administer an oath to the person signing. If the form does not contain a jurat, then no oath is required.

Over the years the DMV has produced several different versions of the title form. Five different versions follow as examples—you may encounter any of them. For simplicity, they are referred to here as Forms I, II, III, IV, and V.

---

55. G.S. 20-112.

Form I

Form I has recently been adopted by the DMV.

Federal and State law requires that you state the mileage in connection with the transfer of ownership. Failure to complete or providing a false statement may result in fines and/or imprisonment.

A   FIRST RE-ASSIGNMENT OF TITLE BY REGISTERED OWNER

The undersigned hereby certifies that the vehicle described in this title has been transferred to the following printed name and address:

Name of Buyer:

Address of Buyer:

I, seller(s) certify to the best of my knowledge that the odometer reading is the actual mileage of the vehicle unless one of the following statements is checked.

☐ 1. The mileage stated is in excess of its mechanical limits.
☐ 2. The odometer reading is not the actual mileage.

ODOMETER READING (No tenths)   WARNING ODOMETER DISCREPANCY

Seller(s) Signature
Seller(s) Hand Printed Name
Notary Public
Acknowledged before me this _____ day of _____, 20 ____.
My Commission expires _____   (SEAL)
Buyer(s) Signature
Buyer(s) Hand Printed Name

To my knowledge the vehicle described herein:
Yes ☐ No ☐ Has been involved in a collision or other occurrence to the extent that the cost to repair exceeds 25% of fair market value.
Yes ☐ No ☐ Has been a flood vehicle.
Yes ☐ No ☐ Has been a reconstructed or a salvage vehicle.

Date vehicle delivered to purchaser _____

B   FIRST RE-ASSIGNMENT OF TITLE BY DEALER

The undersigned hereby certifies that the vehicle described in this title has been transferred to the following printed name and address:

Name of Buyer:

Address of Buyer:

I, seller(s) certify to the best of my knowledge that the odometer reading is the actual mileage of the vehicle unless one of the following statements is checked.

☐ 1. The mileage stated is in excess of its mechanical limits.
☐ 2. The odometer reading is not the actual mileage.

ODOMETER READING (No tenths)   WARNING ODOMETER DISCREPANCY

Dealer Name _____   Dealer# _____
Dealer(s) Signature
Dealer(s) Hand Printed Name
Notary Public
Acknowledged before me this _____ day of _____, 20 ____.
My Commission expires _____   (SEAL)
Buyer(s) Signature
Buyer(s) Hand Printed Name

To my knowledge the vehicle described herein:
Yes ☐ No ☐ Has been involved in a collision or other occurrence to the extent that the cost to repair exceeds 25% of fair market value.
Yes ☐ No ☐ Has been a flood vehicle.
Yes ☐ No ☐ Has been a reconstructed or a salvage vehicle.

Date vehicle delivered to purchaser _____

C   PURCHASER S APPLICATION FOR NEW CERTIFICATE OF TITLE

The undersigned purchaser of the vehicle described on the face of this certificate, hereby makes application for a new certificate of title and certifies that said vehicle is subject to the following named liens and none other and that the information contained herein is true and accurate to my best knowledge and belief.

OWNER(S)
Owner 1 DL# _____
Full Legal name of Owner (First, Middle, Last, Suffix) or Company

Owner 2 DL# _____
Full Legal name of Owner (First, Middle, Last, Suffix) or Company

Residence Address _____

City _____ State _____ Zip Code _____ Tax County _____

Mail Address (if different from above) _____

FIRST LIEN	SECOND LIEN
Date of Lien _____ Account # _____ Lienholder ID _____	Date of Lien _____ Account # _____ Lienholder ID _____
Lienholder Name _____	Lienholder Name _____
Address _____	Address _____
City _____ State _____ Zip Code _____	City _____ State _____ Zip Code _____

I certify for the motor vehicle described herein that I have financial responsibility as required by law.

Insurance Company Authorized in NC _____   Policy Number _____   ODOMETER READING

Signature of Owner(s) _____

Acknowledged before me this _____ day of _____, 20 ____.   My commission expires _____

Notary Public _____   (SEAL)

NOTE: RETAIL PURCHASER MUST APPLY FOR NEW TITLE WITHIN 28 DAYS AFTER PURCHASE OR PAY STATUTORY PENALTY. ALTERATION OR ERASURES WILL VOID THIS TITLE.

(Form I) Part A. First Re-assignment of Title by Registered Owner

Federal and State law requires that you state the mileage in connection with the transfer of ownership. Failure to complete or providing a false statement may result in fines and/or imprisonment.

A   **FIRST RE-ASSIGNMENT OF TITLE BY REGISTERED OWNER**

The undersigned hereby certifies that the vehicle described in this title has been transferred to the following printed name and address:

Name of Buyer: ____ (A) _____

Address of Buyer: ____ (B) _____

I, seller(s) certify to the best of my knowledge that the odometer reading is the actual mileage of the vehicle unless one of the following statements is checked.

❏ 1. The mileage stated is in excess of its mechanical limits.
❏ 2. The odometer reading is not the actual mileage.

(C)
ODOMETER READING
(No tenths)   **WARNING   ODOMETER DISCREPANCY**

To my knowledge the vehicle described herein:
(D) Yes ❏ No ❏ Has been involved in a collision or other occurrence to the extent that the cost to repair exceeds 25% of fair market value.
Yes ❏ No ❏ Has been a flood vehicle.
Yes ❏ No ❏ Has been a reconstructed or a salvage vehicle.

Date vehicle delivered to purchaser ____ (E) ____

Seller(s) Signature ____ (F) ____
Seller(s) Hand Printed Name ____ (G) ____
Notary Public ____ (H) ____
Acknowledged before me this (I) day of (J) , 20 (K)
My Commission expires (L)   *(SEAL)*
Buyer(s) Signature (M)
Buyer(s) Hand Printed Name (N)

B   **FIRST RE-ASSIGNMENT OF TITLE BY DEALER**

A. Full typed or printed name of buyer.
B. Buyer's street address and city or town.
C. Odometer reading on date re-assignment of title is executed.
D. Yes and no questions concerning condition of vehicle that must be answered.
E. Date vehicle delivered to purchaser (usually date of title re-assignment).
F. Seller's full signature.
G. Seller's full hand-printed name.

H. Notary's signature as it appears in the seal or stamp.
I. Date notary takes certification.
J. Month notary takes certification.
K. Year notary takes certification.
L. Month, date, and year notary's commission expires.
M. Buyer's full signature.
N. Buyer's full hand-printed name.

Federal and State law requires that you state the mileage in connection with the transfer of ownership. Failure to complete or providing a false statement may result in fines and/or imprisonment.

A   **FIRST RE-ASSIGNMENT OF TITLE BY REGISTERED OWNER**

The undersigned hereby certifies that the vehicle described in this title has been transferred to the following printed name and address:

Name of Buyer: _Don's Used Cars_

Address of Buyer: _305 Monterey, Fayetteville_

I, seller(s) certify to the best of my knowledge that the odometer reading is the actual mileage of the vehicle unless one of the following statements is checked.

❏ 1. The mileage stated is in excess of its mechanical limits.
❏ 2. The odometer reading is not the actual mileage.

33,456
ODOMETER READING
(No tenths)   **WARNING   ODOMETER DISCREPANCY**

To my knowledge the vehicle described herein:
Yes ❏ No ☒ Has been involved in a collision or other occurrence to the extent that the cost to repair exceeds 25% of fair market value.
Yes ❏ No ☒ Has been a flood vehicle.
Yes ❏ No ☒ Has been a reconstructed or a salvage vehicle.

Date vehicle delivered to purchaser _12-15-2003_

Seller(s) Signature _Kelly Brandon Simpson_
Seller(s) Hand Printed Name _Kelly Brandon Simpson_
Notary Public _Barbara J. Jones_
Acknowledged before me this _15th_ day of _December_ , 20 _03_
My Commission expires _3-15-2005_   *(SEAL)*
Buyer(s) Signature _Don's Used Cars by Tom Smith_
Buyer(s) Hand Printed Name _Don's Used Cars, by Tom Smith_

B   **FIRST RE-ASSIGNMENT OF TITLE BY DEALER**

(Form I) Part B. First Re-assignment of Title by Dealer

FIRST RE-ASSIGNMENT OF TITLE BY DEALER

The undersigned hereby certifies that the vehicle described in this title has been transferred to the following printed name and address:

Name of Buyer: (A)

Address of Buyer: (B)

I, seller(s) certify to the best of my knowledge that the odometer reading is the actual mileage of the vehicle unless one of the following statements is checked.

(C) ODOMETER READING *(No tenths)*

☐ 1. The mileage stated is in excess of its mechanical limits.
☐ 2. The odometer reading is not the actual mileage. WARNING ODOMETER DISCREPANCY

To my knowledge the vehicle described herein:
Yes ☐ No ☐ Has been involved in a collision or other occurrence to the extent that the cost to repair exceeds 25% of fair market value.
Yes ☐ No ☐ Has been a flood vehicle.
Yes ☐ No ☐ Has been a reconstructed or a salvage vehicle. (D)

Date vehicle delivered to purchaser (E)

Dealer Name (F) Dealer# (G)
Dealer(s) Signature (H)
Dealer(s) Hand Printed N (I)
Notary Public (J)
Acknowledged before me this (K) of (L) , 20 (M)
My Commission expires (N) (SEAL)
Buyer(s) Signature (O)
Buyer(s) Hand Printed Name (P)

PURCHASER S APPLICATION FOR NEW CERTIFICATE OF TITLE

A. Full typed or printed name of buyer.
B. Buyer's street address and city or town.
C. Odometer reading on date re-assignment of title is executed.
D. Yes and no questions concerning condition of vehicle that must be answered.
E. Date vehicle delivered to purchaser (usually date of title re-assignment).
F. Full printed or typed name of dealer.
G. Dealer's certificate number.
H. Full signature of dealer's agent (omission of this item will cause title application to be rejected).
I. Full hand-printed name of agent signing for dealership.
J. Notary's signature as it appears in the seal or stamp.
K. Date notary takes certification.
L. Month notary takes certification.
M. Year notary takes certification.
N. Month, date, and year notary's commission expires.
O. Buyer's full signature.
P. Buyer's full hand-printed name.

FIRST RE-ASSIGNMENT OF TITLE BY DEALER

The undersigned hereby certifies that the vehicle described in this title has been transferred to the following printed name and address:

Name of Buyer: Jennifer Hatch Boone

Address of Buyer: 238 Forest Drive, Wendell, NC

I, seller(s) certify to the best of my knowledge that the odometer reading is the actual mileage of the vehicle unless one of the following statements is checked.

33,973 ODOMETER READING *(No tenths)*

☐ 1. The mileage stated is in excess of its mechanical limits.
☐ 2. The odometer reading is not the actual mileage. WARNING ODOMETER DISCREPANCY

To my knowledge the vehicle described herein:
Yes ☐ No ☒ Has been involved in a collision or other occurrence to the extent that the cost to repair exceeds 25% of fair market value.
Yes ☐ No ☒ Has been a flood vehicle.
Yes ☐ No ☒ Has been a reconstructed or a salvage vehicle.

Date vehicle delivered to purchaser 1-5-2004

Dealer Name Don's Used Cars Dealer# 45622
Dealer(s) Signature Don's Used Cars by Tom Smith
Dealer(s) Hand Printed Name Don's Used Cars, by Tom Smith
Notary Public Mary Ann Ray
Acknowledged before me this 6th day of January , 20 04
My Commission expires 12-7-2004 (SEAL)
Buyer(s) Signature Jennifer Hatch Boone
Buyer(s) Hand Printed Name Jennifer Hatch Boone

PURCHASER S APPLICATION FOR NEW CERTIFICATE OF TITLE

(Form I) Part C. Purchaser's Application for New Certificate of Title

A. Purchaser's driver's license number.
B. Full typed or printed name of purchaser as shown on driver's license.
C. Purchaser's street address.
D. Purchaser's city or town.
E. Purhaser's state (which should be only North Carolina).
F. Purchaser's zip code.
G. Purchaser's tax county.
H. Purchaser's mailing address if different from residence or business address.
I. Date first lien created.
J. Account number provided by lienholder.
K. Lienholder's identification number.
L. Holder of first lien.

M. Lienholder's address.
N. Lienholder's city.
O. Lienholder's state.
P. Lienholder's zip code.
Q. Full typed or printed name of insurance company issuing policy that insures vehicle.
R. Insurance policy number.
S. Odometer reading on date application signed.
T. Purchaser's full signature.
U. Date notary takes certification.
V. Month notary takes certification.
W. Year notary takes certification.
X. Month, date, and year notary's commission expires.
Y. Notary's signature as it appears in the seal or stamp.

Example: Kelly Simpson sells his 2000 Honda to Don's Used Cars. Don's Used Cars sells the car to Jennifer Boone, and Boone applies for a certificate of title in her name. The sale to Boone and her application for a certificate of title are certified before the same notary in Fayetteville, Cumberland County.

Form II

Form II is similar to Form I but has been in use for several years. Note that in Part A of this form the notary is taking the acknowledgement of the seller only.

Federal and State law requires that you state the mileage in connection with the transfer of ownership. Failure to complete or providing a false statement may result in fines and/or imprisonment.

A | **ASSIGNMENT OF TITLE BY REGISTERED OWNER**
The undersigned hereby certifies that the vehicle described in this title has been transferred to the following printed name and address:

"I certify to the best of my knowledge that the odometer reading is: _____ **(NO TENTHS)** and reflects the actual mileage of this vehicle unless one of the following statements is checked.
☐ 1. The mileage stated is in excess of its mechanical limits.
☐ 2. The odometer reading is not the actual mileage.   **WARNING—ODOMETER DISCREPANCY**

To my knowledge the vehicle described herein ☐ has been   ☐ has not been involved in collision or other
DATE VEHICLE DELIVERED TO PURCHASER   occurrence to the extent that the cost to repair exceeds 25% of fair market retail value.

Hand Printed Name and
Signature(s) of Seller(s) _____

Acknowledged before me this _____ day of _____, 19 ____ County _____ State _____

Notary Public _____ My Commission expires the _____ day of _____ 19 ____
(SEAL)

"I am aware of the above odometer certification and damage disclosure made by the seller."

Hand Printed Name and
Signature(s) of Buyer(s) _____

B | **FIRST RE-ASSIGNMENT BY DEALER**
The undersigned hereby certifies that the vehicle described in this title has been transferred to the following printed name and address:

"I certify to the best of my knowledge that the odometer reading is: _____ **(NO TENTHS)** and reflects the actual mileage of this vehicle unless one of the following statements is checked.
☐ 1. The mileage stated is in excess of its mechanical limits.
☐ 2. The odometer reading is not the actual mileage.   **WARNING—ODOMETER DISCREPANCY**

To my knowledge the vehicle described herein ☐ has been   ☐ has not been involved in collision or other
DATE VEHICLE DELIVERED TO PURCHASER   occurrence to the extent that the cost to repair exceeds 25% of fair market retail value.

Hand Printed Name and
Signature of Dealer or Agent _____ Dealer's No. _____

Printed Firm Name _____

Acknowledged before me this _____ day of _____, 19 ____ County _____ State _____

Notary Public _____ My Commission expires the _____ day of _____ 19 ____
(SEAL)

"I am aware of the above odometer certification and damage disclosure made by the seller."

Hand Printed Name and
Signature(s) of Buyer(s) _____

C | **PURCHASER'S APPLICATION FOR NEW CERTIFICATE OF TITLE**
THE UNDERSIGNED, PURCHASER OF THE VEHICLE DESCRIBED ON THE FACE OF THIS CERTIFICATE, HEREBY MAKES APPLICATION FOR A NEW CERTIFICATE OF TITLE AND CERTIFIES THAT SAID VEHICLE IS SUBJECT TO THE FOLLOWING NAMED LIENS AND NONE OTHER, AND THAT THE INFORMATION CONTAINED HEREIN IS TRUE AND ACCURATE TO MY BEST KNOWLEDGE AND BELIEF.

OWNER'S CERTIFICATION FOR ELIGIBILITY TO REGISTER

I CERTIFY FOR THE MOTOR VEHICLE DESCRIBED ON THIS TITLE THAT I HAVE FINANCIAL RESPONSIBILITY AS REQUIRED BY LAW.

Print or type full name of insurance company authorized in N.C.—not agency or group

Policy number—If policy not issued, name of agency binding coverage

FIRST LIEN _____ DATE _____

LIENHOLDER _____

STREET OR R.F.D. _____ CITY OR TOWN _____

SECOND LIEN _____ DATE _____

LIENHOLDER _____

STREET OR R.F.D. _____ CITY OR TOWN _____

SIGNATURE OF PURCHASER(S)

D. L. Number	Purchase Price	Odometer Reading (No Tenths)
	$	

FIRST NAME   MIDDLE NAME   LAST NAME

ALL ANSWERS SUPPLIED AND ACKNOWLEDGED BEFORE ME THIS

_____ DAY OF _____ 19 ____

PRINT IN INK OR TYPE NAME EXACTLY AS IT APPEARS ABOVE IN SIGNATURE

MY COMMISSION EXPIRES _____

RESIDENCE ADDRESS _____ **(SEAL)**

POST OFFICE   COUNTY OF RESIDENCE   ZIP CODE

SIGNATURE OF NOTARY PUBLIC IN INK

NOTE: RETAIL PURCHASER MUST APPLY FOR NEW TITLE WITHIN 28 DAYS AFTER PURCHASE OR PAY STATUTORY PENALTY. ALTERATIONS OR ERASURES WILL VOID THIS TITLE

(Form II) Part A. Assignment of Title by Registered Owner

Federal and State law requires that you state the mileage in connection with the transfer of ownership. Failure to complete or providing a false statement may result in fines and/or imprisonment.

A **ASSIGNMENT OF TITLE BY REGISTERED OWNER**

The undersigned hereby certifies that the vehicle described in this title has been transferred to the following printed name and address:

"I certify to the best of my knowledge that the odometer reading is: _____ (NO TENTHS) and reflects the actual mileage of this vehicle unless one of the following statements is checked.
☐ 1. The mileage stated is in excess of its mechanical limits.
☐ 2. The odometer reading is not the actual mileage. **WARNING—ODOMETER DISCREPANCY**

DATE VEHICLE DELIVERED TO PURCHASER — To my knowledge the vehicle described herein ☐ has been ☐ has not been involved in collision or other occurrence to the extent that the cost to repair exceeds 25% of fair market retail value.

Hand Printed Name and Signature(s) of Seller(s) _____

Acknowledged before me this _____ day of _____ 19___ County _____

Notary Public _____ My Commission expires the _____ day of _____ 19___ (SEAL)

"I am aware of the above odometer certification and damage disclosure made by the seller."

Hand Printed Name and Signature(s) of Buyer(s) _____

B **FIRST RE-ASSIGNMENT BY DEALER**

The undersigned hereby certifies that the vehicle described in this title has been transferred to the following printed name and address:

A. Full typed or printed name of purchaser.

B. Purchaser's street address and city or town.

C. Odometer reading on date assignment of title is executed.

D. Date vehicle delivered to purchaser (usually date of title assignment).

E. Seller's full hand-printed name.

F. Seller's full signature.

G. Date notary takes certification.

H. Month notary takes certification.

I. Year notary takes certification.

J. County in which assignment executed.

K. State in which assignment executed.

L. Notary's signature as it appears in the seal or stamp.

M. Date notary's commission expires.

N. Month notary's commission expires.

O. Year notary's commission expires.

P. Buyer's full hand-printed name.

Q. Buyer's full signature.

Federal and State law requires that you state the mileage in connection with the transfer of ownership. Failure to complete or providing a false statement may result in fines and/or imprisonment.

A **ASSIGNMENT OF TITLE BY REGISTERED OWNER**

The undersigned hereby certifies that the vehicle described in this title has been transferred to the following printed name and address:

M&M Auto Sales, Inc., 5001 Big Bypass, New Bern, NC

"I certify to the best of my knowledge that the odometer reading is: *52,102* (NO TENTHS) and reflects the actual mileage of this vehicle unless one of the following statements is checked.
☐ 1. The mileage stated is in excess of its mechanical limits.
☐ 2. The odometer reading is not the actual mileage. **WARNING—ODOMETER DISCREPANCY**

April 7, 2004
DATE VEHICLE DELIVERED TO PURCHASER — To my knowledge the vehicle described herein ☐ has been ☐ has not been involved in collision or other occurrence to the extent that the cost to repair exceeds 25% of fair market retail value.

Hand Printed Name and Signature(s) of Seller(s) *SALLY MAY NELSON* *Sally May Nelson*

Acknowledged before me this *7th* day of *April* 19*2004* County *CRAVEN* State *NC*

Notary Public *Felicia Grant* My Commission expires the *12* day of *DEC 12 2005* (SEAL)

"I am aware of the above odometer certification and damage disclosure made by the seller."

Hand Printed Name and Signature(s) of Buyer(s) *M&M Auto Sales, Inc., by Jerry Rigg*

B **FIRST RE-ASSIGNMENT BY DEALER**

The undersigned hereby certifies that the vehicle described in this title has been transferred to the following printed name and address:

(Form II) Part B. First Re-assignment by Dealer

B		FIRST RE-ASSIGNMENT BY DEALER	

The undersigned hereby certifies that the vehicle described in this title has been transferred to the following printed name and address:

(A) (C) (B)

"I certify to the best of my knowledge that the odometer reading is: _____ **(NO TENTHS)** and reflects the actual mileage of this vehicle unless one of the following statements is checked.
☐ 1. The mileage stated is in excess of its mechanical limits.
☐ 2. The odometer reading is not the actual mileage.   **WARNING—ODOMETER DISCREPANCY**

(D)

DATE VEHICLE DELIVERED TO PURCHASER   To my knowledge the vehicle described herein ☐ has been ☐ has not been involved in collision or other occurrence to the extent that the cost to repair exceeds 25% of fair market retail value.

Hand Printed Name and Signature of Dealer or Agent _____ (E) (F) Dealer's No. _____ (G)

Printed Firm Name _____ (H)

Acknowledged before me this _____ (I) day of _____ (J) 19 _____ (K) County (L) State (M)

Notary Public _____ (N)   My Commission expires the _____ (O) day of _____ (P) 19 _____ (Q)
(SEAL)

"I am aware of the above odometer certification and damage disclosure made by the seller."

Hand Printed Name and Signature(s) of Buyer(s) _____ (R) (S)

C	PURCHASER'S APPLICATION FOR NEW CERTIFICATE OF TITLE

THE UNDERSIGNED, PURCHASER OF THE VEHICLE DESCRIBED ON THE FACE OF THIS CERTIFICATE, HEREBY MAKES APPLICATION FOR A NEW CERTIFICATE OF TITLE AND CERTIFIES THAT SAID VEHICLE IS SUBJECT TO THE FOLLOWING NAMED LIENS AND NONE OTHER, AND THAT THE INFORMATION CONTAINED HEREIN IS

A. Full typed or printed name of purchaser.

B. Purchaser's street address and city or town.

C. Odometer reading at date of title re-assignment.

D. Date vehicle delivered by dealer to new owner (usually date of title re-assignment).

E. Full hand-printed name of agent signing for dealership.

F. Full signature of dealer's agent (omission of this item will cause title application to be rejected).

G. Dealer's certificate number.

H. Full printed or typed name of dealer.

I. Date notary takes certification.

J. Month notary takes certification.

K. Year notary takes certification.

L. County in which re-assignment executed.

M. State in which re-assignment executed.

N. Notary's signature as it appears in the seal or stamp.

O. Date notary's commission expires.

P. Month notary's commission expires.

Q. Year notary's commission expires.

R. Buyer's full hand-printed name.

S. Buyer's full signature.

B		FIRST RE-ASSIGNMENT BY DEALER	

The undersigned hereby certifies that the vehicle described in this title has been transferred to the following printed name and address:
Charles Taylor Smith, 10 Springs Street, New Bern, NC

"I certify to the best of my knowledge that the odometer reading is: 57702 **(NO TENTHS)** and reflects the actual mileage of this vehicle unless one of the following statements is checked.
☐ 1. The mileage stated is in excess of its mechanical limits.
☐ 2. The odometer reading is not the actual mileage.   **WARNING—ODOMETER DISCREPANCY**

April 25, 2004
DATE VEHICLE DELIVERED TO PURCHASER   To my knowledge the vehicle described herein ☐ has been ☑ has not been involved in collision or other occurrence to the extent that the cost to repair exceeds 25% of fair market retail value.

Hand Printed Name and Signature of Dealer or Agent Grant Hughes   Grant Hughes   Dealer's No. 38071

Printed Firm Name M & M Auto Sales, Inc.

Acknowledged before me this 25th day of April 19 2004 County Craven   State NC

Notary Public Margret L. Riney   My Commission expires the 10th day of Jan. 19 2006
(SEAL)

"I am aware of the above odometer certification and damage disclosure made by the seller."

Hand Printed Name and Signature(s) of Buyer(s) Charles Taylor Smith   Charles Taylor Smith

C	PURCHASER'S APPLICATION FOR NEW CERTIFICATE OF TITLE

THE UNDERSIGNED, PURCHASER OF THE VEHICLE DESCRIBED ON THE FACE OF THIS CERTIFICATE, HEREBY MAKES APPLICATION FOR A NEW CERTIFICATE OF TITLE AND CERTIFIES THAT SAID VEHICLE IS SUBJECT TO THE FOLLOWING NAMED LIENS AND NONE OTHER, AND THAT THE INFORMATION CONTAINED HEREIN IS TRUE AND ACCURATE TO MY BEST KNOWLEDGE AND BELIEF.

(Form II) Part C. Purchaser's Application for New Certificate of Title

A. Full typed or printed name of insurance company issuing policy that insures vehicle.

B. Insurance policy number.

C. Date first lien created.

D. Holder of first lien.

E. Lienholder's street or box address.

F. Lienholder's city or town.

G. Purchaser's full signature.

H. Full typed or printed name of purchaser exactly as it appears on the signature line.

I. Purchaser's street address.

J. Purchaser's city or town.

K. Purchaser's county of residence.

L. Purchaser's zip code.

M. Purchaser's driver's license number.

N. Amount purchaser paid for vehicle.

O. Odometer reading on date application signed.

P. Date notary takes certification.

Q. Month notary takes certification.

R. Year notary takes certification.

S. Date, month, and year notary's commission expires.

T. Notary's signature as it appears in the seal or stamp.

Example: Sally Nelson sells her 2002 Toyota to M & M Auto Sales, Inc. M & M sells the car to Charles Smith, and Smith applies for a certificate of title in his name. The sale to Smith and his application for a certificate of title are certified before the same notary in New Bern, Craven County.

Form III

Form III is a title certificate that has been in use for several years. Note that in Part A of this form the notary is taking the acknowledgment of the seller only. In Part C the notary is required to provide his or her address, unlike on the other title certificate forms.

Federal and State law requires that you state the mileage in connection with the transfer of ownership. Failure to complete or providing a false statement may result in fines and/or imprisonment.

A ASSIGNMENT OF TITLE BY REGISTERED OWNER
The undersigned hereby certifies that the vehicle described in this title has been transferred to the following printed name and address:

"I certify to the best of my knowledge that the odometer reading is: _____ (NO TENTHS) and reflects the actual mileage of this vehicle unless one of the following statements is checked.
☐ 1. The mileage stated is in excess of its mechanical limits.
☐ 2. The odometer reading is not the actual mileage.   **WARNING—ODOMETER DISCREPANCY**

To my knowledge the vehicle described herein ☐ has been ☐ has not been involved in collision or other
DATE VEHICLE DELIVERED TO PURCHASER   occurrence to the extent that the cost to repair exceeds 25% of fair market retail value.

Hand Printed Name and
Signature(s) of Seller(s) _____

Subscribed and Sworn to before me in my presence this _____ day of _____, 19_____ County _____ State _____

Notary Public _____ My Commission expires the _____ day of _____ 19 _____
(SEAL)
"I am aware of the above odometer certification and damage disclosure made by the seller."

Hand Printed Name and
Signature(s) of Buyer(s) _____

B FIRST RE-ASSIGNMENT BY DEALER
The undersigned hereby certifies that the vehicle described in this title has been transferred to the following printed name and address:

"I certify to the best of my knowledge that the odometer reading is: _____ (NO TENTHS) and reflects the actual mileage of this vehicle unless one of the following statements is checked.
☐ 1. The mileage stated is in excess of its mechanical limits.
☐ 2. The odometer reading is not the actual mileage.   **WARNING—ODOMETER DISCREPANCY**

To my knowledge the vehicle described herein ☐ has been ☐ has not been involved in collision or other
DATE VEHICLE DELIVERED TO PURCHASER   occurrence to the extent that the cost to repair exceeds 25% of fair market retail value.

Hand Printed Name and
Signature of Dealer or Agent _____ Dealer's No. _____

Printed Firm Name _____

Subscribed and Sworn to before me in my presence this _____ day of _____, 19_____ County _____ State _____

Notary Public _____ My Commission expires the _____ day of _____ 19 _____
(SEAL)
"I am aware of the above odometer certification and damage disclosure made by the seller."

Hand Printed Name and
Signature(s) of Buyer(s) _____

C PURCHASER'S APPLICATION FOR NEW CERTIFICATE OF TITLE
THE UNDERSIGNED, PURCHASER OF THE VEHICLE DESCRIBED ON THE FACE OF THIS CERTIFICATE, HEREBY MAKES APPLICATION FOR A NEW CERTIFICATE OF TITLE AND CERTIFIES THAT SAID VEHICLE IS SUBJECT TO THE FOLLOWING NAMED LIENS AND NONE OTHER, AND THAT THE INFORMATION CONTAINED HEREIN IS TRUE AND ACCURATE TO MY BEST KNOWLEDGE AND BELIEF.

OWNER'S CERTIFICATION FOR ELIGIBILITY TO REGISTER

I CERTIFY FOR THE MOTOR VEHICLE DESCRIBED ON THIS TITLE THAT I HAVE FINANCIAL RESPONSIBILITY AS REQUIRED BY LAW.

Print or type full name of insurance company authorized in N.C.—not agency or group

Policy number—If policy not issued, name of agency binding coverage

FIRST LIEN _____ DATE _____

LIENHOLDER _____

STREET OR R.F.D. _____ CITY OR TOWN _____

SECOND LIEN _____ DATE _____

LIENHOLDER _____

STREET OR R.F.D. _____ CITY OR TOWN _____

SIGNATURE OF PURCHASER(S)

D. L. Number	Purchase Price	Odometer Reading (No Tenths)
	$	

FIRST NAME   MIDDLE NAME   LAST NAME

ALL ANSWERS SUPPLIED AND COMPLETELY SUBSCRIBED AND SWORN TO BEFORE

ME THIS _____ DAY OF _____ 19 _____

MY COMMISSION EXPIRES _____

_____ (SEAL)
SIGNATURE OF NOTARY PUBLIC IN INK

PRINT IN INK OR TYPE NAME EXACTLY AS IT APPEARS ABOVE IN SIGNATURE

RESIDENCE ADDRESS

POST OFFICE   COUNTY OF RESIDENCE   ZIP CODE   ADDRESS OF NOTARY PUBLIC

NOTE: RETAIL PURCHASER MUST APPLY FOR NEW TITLE WITHIN 28 DAYS AFTER PURCHASE OR PAY STATUTORY PENALTY. ALTERATIONS OR ERASURES WILL VOID THIS TITLE

(Form III) Part A. Assignment of Title by Registered Owner

Federal and State law requires that you state the mileage in connection with the transfer of ownership. Failure to complete or providing a false statement may result in fines and/or imprisonment.

A **ASSIGNMENT OF TITLE BY REGISTERED OWNER**

The undersigned hereby certifies that the vehicle described in this title has been transferred to the following printed name rnd address:

Ⓐ Ⓑ

"I certify to the best of my knowledge that the odometer reading is: _____ Ⓒ _____ **(NO TENTHS)** and reflects the actual mileage of this vehicle unless one of the following statements is checked.

☐ 1. The mileage stated is in excess of its mechanical limits.
☐ 2. The odometer reading is not the actual mileage. **WARNING—ODOMETER DISCREPANCY**

Ⓓ To my knowledge the vehicle described herein ☐ has been ☐ has not been involved in collision or other
DATE VEHICLE DELIVERED TO PURCHASER occurrence to the extent that the cost to repair exceeds 25% of fair market retail value.

Hand Printed Name and
Signature(s) of Seller(s) Ⓔ Ⓕ Ⓚ

Subscribed and Sworn to before Ⓛ my presence this ___ Ⓖ ___ day of ___ Ⓗ ___ 19 Ⓘ ___ County ___ Ⓙ ___ M Ⓝ Ⓞ

Notary Public _____ My Commission expires the ___ Ⓜ ___ day of ___ 19
(SEAL)

"I am aware of the above odometer certification and damage disclosure made by the seller."

Hand Printed Name and
Signature(s) of Buyer(s) Ⓟ Ⓠ

B **FIRST RE-ASSIGNMENT BY DEALER**

A. Full typed or printed name of purchaser.

B. Purchaser's street address and city or town.

C. Odometer reading on date assignment of title is executed.

D. Date vehicle delivered to purchaser (usually date of title assignment).

E. Seller's full hand-printed name.

F. Seller's full signature.

G. Date notary takes certification.

H. Month notary takes certification.

I. Year notary takes certification.

J. County in which assignment executed.

K. State in which assignment executed.

L. Notary's signature as it appears in the seal or stamp.

M. Date notary's commission expires.

N. Month notary's commission expires.

O. Year notary's commission expires.

P. Buyer's full hand-printed name.

Q. Buyer's full signature.

Federal and State law requires that you state the mileage in connection with the transfer of ownership. Failure to complete or providing a false statement may result in fines and/or imprisonment.

A **ASSIGNMENT OF TITLE BY REGISTERED OWNER**

The undersigned hereby certifies that the vehicle described in this title has been transferred to the following printed name rnd address:

FRIENDLY USED CARS, 123 MAIN DRAG, BURGAW

"I certify to the best of my knowledge that the odometer reading is: ___ *41060* ___ **(NO TENTHS)** and reflects the actual mileage of this vehicle unless one of the following statements is checked.

☐ 1. The mileage stated is in excess of its mechanical limits.
☐ 2. The odometer reading is not the actual mileage. **WARNING—ODOMETER DISCREPANCY**

4/1/2004
DATE VEHICLE DELIVERED TO PURCHASER To my knowledge the vehicle described herein ☐ has been ☐ has not been involved in collision or other occurrence to the extent that the cost to repair exceeds 25% of fair market retail value.

Hand Printed Name and
Signature(s) of Seller(s) *CARY JOE SIMPSON* *Cary Joe Simpson*

Subscribed and Sworn to before me in my presence this *1st* day of *April* 19 *2004* County *PENDER* State *NC*

Notary Public *Michael X. Soileau* My Commission expires the *10th* day of *JUNE* 19 *2007*
(SEAL)

"I am aware of the above odometer certification and damage disclosure made by the seller."

Hand Printed Name and
Signature(s) of Buyer(s) *FRIENDLY USED CARS by Otto Venator*

B **FIRST RE-ASSIGNMENT BY DEALER**

(Form III) Part B. First Re-assignment by Dealer

B | **FIRST RE-ASSIGNMENT BY DEALER**

The undersigned her~~e~~ rtifies that the vehicle described in this title has been transferred to the following d name and address:

"I certify to the best of my knowledge that the odometer reading is: _____ (NO TENTHS) and reflects the actual mileage of this vehicle unless one of the following statements is checked.

☐ 1. The mileage stated is in excess of its mechanical limits.
☐ 2. The odometer reading is not the actual mileage.   **WARNING—ODOMETER DISCREPANCY**

To my knowledge the vehicle described herein ☐ has been ☐ has not been involved in collision or other
DATE VEHICLE DELIVERED TO PURCHASER   occurrence to the extent that the cost to repair exceeds 25% of fair market retail value.

Hand Printed Name and
Signature of Dealer or Agent _____   Dealer's No. _____

Printed Firm Name _____

Subscribed and Sworn to before me in my presence this ___ day of ___ 19 ___ County _____ State _____

Notary Public _____   My Commission expires the ___ day of ___ 19 ___
(SEAL)

"I am aware of the above odometer certification and damage disclosure made by the seller."

Hand Printed Name and
Signature(s) of Buyer(s) _____

C | **PURCHASER'S APPLICATION FOR NEW CERTIFICATE OF TITLE**

THE UNDERSIGNED, PURCHASER OF THE VEHICLE DESCRIBED ON THE FACE OF THIS CERTIFICATE, HEREBY MAKES APPLICATION FOR A NEW CERTIFICATE OF TITLE AND CERTIFIES THAT SAID VEHICLE IS SUBJECT TO THE FOLLOWING NAMED LIENS AND NONE OTHER, AND THAT THE INFORMATION CONTAINED HEREIN IS

A. Full typed or printed name of purchaser.

B. Purchaser's street address and city or town.

C. Odometer reading at date of title re-assignment.

D. Date vehicle delivered by dealer to new owner (usually date of title re-assignment).

E. Full hand-printed name of agent signing for dealership.

F. Full signature of dealer's agent (omission of this item will cause title application to be rejected).

G. Dealer's certificate number.

H. Full printed or typed name of dealer.

I. Date notary takes certification.

J. Month notary takes certification.

K. Year notary takes certification.

L. County in which re-assignment is executed.

M. State in which re-assignment is executed.

N. Notary's signature as it appears in the seal or stamp.

O. Date notary's commission expires.

P. Month notary's commission expires.

Q. Year notary's commission expires.

R. Buyer's full hand-printed name.

S. Buyer's full signature.

B | **FIRST RE-ASSIGNMENT BY DEALER**

The undersigned hereby certifies that the vehicle described in this title has been transferred to the following printed name and address:

BOBBY Wayne King, RR1, BOX 750 BURGAW

"I certify to the best of my knowledge that the odometer reading is: *41141* (NO TENTHS) and reflects the actual mileage of this vehicle unless one of the following statements is checked.

☐ 1. The mileage stated is in excess of its mechanical limits.
☐ 2. The odometer reading is not the actual mileage.   **WARNING—ODOMETER DISCREPANCY**

5/1/2004
DATE VEHICLE DELIVERED TO PURCHASER   To my knowledge the vehicle described herein ☐ has been ☒ has not been involved in collision or other occurrence to the extent that the cost to repair exceeds 25% of fair market retail value.

Hand Printed Name and
Signature of Dealer or Agent *Michelle Morris   Michelle Morris*   Dealer's No. *T1056*

Printed Firm Name *FRIENDLY USED CARS*

Subscribed and Sworn to before me in my presence this *1st* day of *May 2004* County *PENDER* State *NC*

Notary Public *Samantha McDoochy*   My Commission expires the *15th* day of *July 2007*
(SEAL)

"I am aware of the above odometer certification and damage disclosure made by the seller."

Hand Printed Name and
Signature(s) of Buyer(s) *BOBBY Wayne King   Bobby Wayne King*

C | **PURCHASER'S APPLICATION FOR NEW CERTIFICATE OF TITLE**

THE UNDERSIGNED, PURCHASER OF THE VEHICLE DESCRIBED ON THE FACE OF THIS CERTIFICATE, HEREBY MAKES APPLICATION FOR A NEW CERTIFICATE OF TITLE AND CERTIFIES THAT SAID VEHICLE IS SUBJECT TO THE FOLLOWING NAMED LIENS AND NONE OTHER, AND THAT THE INFORMATION CONTAINED HEREIN IS TRUE AND ACCURATE TO MY BEST KNOWLEDGE AND BELIEF.

OWNER'S CERTIFICATION FOR ELIGIBILITY TO REGISTER   FIRST LIEN   DATE *5/1/2004*

(Form III) Part C. Purchaser's Application for New Certificate of Title

A. Full typed or printed name of insurance company issuing policy that insures vehicle.
B. Insurance policy number.
C. Date first lien created.
D. Holder of first lien.
E. Lienholder's street or box address.
F. Lienholder's city or town.
G. Purchaser's full signature.
H. Full typed or printed name of purchaser exactly as it appears on the signature line.
I. Purchaser's street address.
J. Purchaser's city or town.
K. Purchaser's county of residence.
L. Purchaser's zip code.
M. Purchaser's driver's license number.
N. Amount purchaser paid for vehicle.
O. Odometer reading on date application signed.
P. Date notary takes certification.
Q. Month notary takes certification.
R. Year notary takes certification.
S. Date, month, and year notary's commission expires.
T. Notary's signature as it appears in the seal or stamp.
U. Notary's address, city, and state.

Example: Cary Joe Simpson sells his 2001 Buick to Friendly Used Cars. Friendly sells the car to Bobby Wayne King, and King applies for a new certificate of title in his name. The transactions are all certified before different Pender County notaries, but all take place in the town of Burgaw.

Form IV

Form IV is a title certificate that has been in use for several years by the DMV. It consists of two sections: Part A, for the assignment of titles by the current registered owner, and Part B, for re-assignment by a registered dealer. Note that in Part A the notary is taking the acknowledgment of the seller only. The purchaser's application for a new title must be made on the MVR-1 (see Form V).

A

ASSIGNMENT OF TITLE BY REGISTERED OWNER

FOR VALUE RECEIVED, THE UNDERSIGNED HEREBY SELLS, ASSIGNS OR TRANSFERS THE VEHICLE DESCRIBED ON THE REVERSE SIDE OF THIS CERTIFICATE UNTO THE PURCHASER WHOSE NAME APPEARS IN THIS BLOCK AND HEREBY WARRANTS THE TITLE TO SAID VEHICLE AND CERTIFIES THAT AT THE TIME OF DELIVERY THE SAME IS SUBJECT TO THE LIENS OR ENCUMBRANCES NAMED IN THE PURCHASER'S APPLICATION FOR NEW CERTIFICATE OF TITLE AND NONE OTHER

PURCHASER'S FIRST, MIDDLE AND LAST NAMES (PRINT IN INK OR TYPE)   STREET OR R.F.D.   CITY OR TOWN

(FEDERAL AND STATE REGULATIONS REQUIRE YOU TO STATE THE ODOMETER MILEAGE UPON TRANSFER OF OWNERSHIP (G. S. 20-347).)

I CERTIFY TO THE BEST OF MY KNOWLEDGE THAT THE ODOMETER READING IS | Odometer Reading | AND REFLECTS THE ACTUAL MILEAGE OF THE VEHICLE UNLESS ONE OR MORE OF THE FOLLOWING STATEMENTS | | IS CHECKED:
☐ 1. THE AMOUNT OF MILEAGE STATED IS IN EXCESS OF 99,999 MILES OR
☐ 2. THE ODOMETER READING IS NOT THE ACTUAL MILEAGE AND SHOULD NOT BE RELIED UPON
☐ 3. THE ODOMETER WAS ALTERED FOR REPAIR OR REPLACEMENT PURPOSES BY _____

ON _____ AND APPROXIMATELY _____ MILES WERE REMOVED BY THE ALTERATION

PURCHASER'S SIGNATURE

_____
DATE VEHICLE DELIVERED TO PURCHASER

ALL ANSWERS SUPPLIED AND COMPLETELY SUBSCRIBED AND SWORN
TO BEFORE ME THIS _____ DAY OF _____
19_____

_____
SELLER'S SIGNATURE

MY COMMISSION EXPIRES _____

_____ (SEAL)
SIGNATURE OF NOTARY PUBLIC IN INK

B

RE-ASSIGNMENT OF TITLE BY REGISTERED DEALER

FOR VALUE RECEIVED, THE UNDERSIGNED HEREBY SELLS, ASSIGNS OR TRANSFERS THE VEHICLE DESCRIBED ON THE REVERSE SIDE OF THIS CERTIFICATE UNTO THE PURCHASER WHOSE NAME APPEARS IN THIS BLOCK AND HEREBY WARRANTS THE TITLE TO SAID VEHICLE AND CERTIFIES THAT AT THE TIME OF DELIVERY THE SAME IS SUBJECT TO THE LIENS OR ENCUMBRANCES NAMED IN THE PURCHASER'S APPLICATION FOR NEW CERTIFICATE OF TITLE AND NONE OTHER

PURCHASER'S FIRST, MIDDLE AND LAST NAMES (PRINT IN INK OR TYPE)   STREET OR R.F.D.   CITY OR TOWN

(FEDERAL AND STATE REGULATIONS REQUIRE YOU TO STATE THE ODOMETER MILEAGE UPON TRANSFER OF OWNERSHIP (G. S. 20-347).)

I CERTIFY TO THE BEST OF MY KNOWLEDGE THAT THE ODOMETER READING IS | Odometer Reading | AND REFLECTS THE ACTUAL MILEAGE OF THE VEHICLE UNLESS ONE OR MORE OF THE FOLLOWING STATEMENTS | | IS CHECKED:
☐ 1. THE AMOUNT OF MILEAGE STATED IS IN EXCESS OF 99,999 MILES OR
☐ 2. THE ODOMETER READING IS NOT THE ACTUAL MILEAGE AND SHOULD NOT BE RELIED UPON
☐ 3. THE ODOMETER WAS ALTERED FOR REPAIR OR REPLACEMENT PURPOSES BY _____

ON _____ AND APPROXIMATELY _____ MILES WERE REMOVED BY THE ALTERATION

PURCHASER'S SIGNATURE

_____
DATE VEHICLE DELIVERED TO PURCHASER

ALL ANSWERS SUPPLIED AND COMPLETELY SUBSCRIBED AND SWORN
TO BEFORE ME THIS _____ DAY OF _____
19_____

DEALER'S NAME (TO AGREE WITH LICENSE)   DEALER CERTIFICATE NO.

MY COMMISSION EXPIRES _____

BY _____
AUTHORIZED AGENT TO SIGN HERE AFTER ENTERING NAME OF PURCHASER

_____ (SEAL)
SIGNATURE OF NOTARY PUBLIC IN INK

A. ALTERATIONS OR ERASURES WILL VOID THIS TITLE
B. LIEN OR ENCUMBRANCE—ENTER IN OWNER'S APPLICATION FOR TITLE
C. RETAIL PURCHASER MUST APPLY FOR NEW TITLE WITHIN 20 DAYS AFTER PURCHASE OR PAY STATUTORY PENALTY

(Form IV) Part A. Assignment of Title by Registered Owner

A

ASSIGNMENT OF TITLE BY REGISTERED OWNER

FOR VALUE RECEIVED, THE UNDERSIGNED HEREBY SELLS, ASSIGNS OR TRANSFERS THE VEHICLE DESCRIBED ON THE REVERSE SIDE OF THIS CERTIFICATE UNTO THE PURCHASER WHOSE NAME APPEARS IN THIS BLOCK AND HEREBY WARRANTS THE TITLE TO SAID VEHICLE AND CERTIFIES THAT AT THE TIME OF DELIVERY THE SAME IS SUBJECT TO THE LIENS OR ENCUMBRANCES NAMED IN THE PURCHASER'S APPLICATION FOR NEW CERTIFICATE OF TITLE AND NONE OTHER.

(A)   (B)   (C)

PURCHASER'S FIRST, MIDDLE AND LAST NAMES (PRINT IN INK OR TYPE)   STREET OR R.F.D.   CITY OR TOWN

(FEDERAL AND STATE REGULATIONS REQUIRE YOU TO STATE THE ODOMETER MILEAGE UPON TRANSFER OF OWNERSHIP (G. S. 20-347.)

I CERTIFY TO THE BEST OF MY KNOWLEDGE THAT THE ODOMETER READING IS   **Odometer Reading**   AND REFLECTS THE ACTUAL MILEAGE OF THE VEHICLE UNLESS ONE OR MORE OF THE FOLLOWING STATEMENTS   (D)   IS CHECKED.

☐ 1. THE AMOUNT OF MILEAGE STATED IS IN EXCESS OF 99,999 MILES OR
☐ 2. THE ODOMETER READING IS NOT THE ACTUAL MILEAGE AND SHOULD NOT BE RELIED UPON.
☐ 3. THE ODOMETER WAS ALTERED FOR REPAIR OR REPLACEMENT PURPOSES BY

ON _____ AND APPROXIMATELY _____ MILES WERE REMOVED BY THE ALTERATION.

(E)

PURCHASER'S SIGNATURE

(F)

ALL ANSWERS SUPPLIED AND COMPLETELY SUBSCRIBED AND SWORN

DATE VEHICLE DELIVERED TO PURCHASER

TO BEFORE ME THIS _____ (H) _____ DAY OF _____ (I)

(G)

19 (J)

(K)

SELLER'S SIGNATURE

MY COMMISSION EXPIRES

(L) _____ (SEAL)

SIGNATURE OF NOTARY PUBLIC IN INK

B   **RE-ASSIGNMENT OF TITLE BY REGISTERED DEALER**

VOID

A. Full typed or printed name of purchaser.

B. Purchaser's street address.

C. Purchaser's city or town.

D. Odometer reading on date of assignment of title.

E. Purchaser's full signature.

F. Date vehicle delivered to purchaser (usually date title was assigned).

G. Seller's full signature.

H. Date notary takes certification.

I. Month notary takes certification.

J. Year notary takes certification.

K. Month, date, and year notary's commission expires.

L. Notary's signature as it appears in the seal or stamp.

(Form IV) Part B. Re-assignment of Title by Registered Dealer

B

RE-ASSIGNMENT OF TITLE BY REGISTERED DEALER

FOR VALUE RECEIVED, THE UNDERSIGNED HEREBY SELLS, ASSIGNS OR TRANSFERS THE VEHICLE DESCRIBED ON THE REVERSE SIDE OF THIS CERTIFICATE UNTO THE PURCHASER WHOSE NAME APPEARS IN THIS BLOCK AND HEREBY WARRANTS THE TITLE TO SAID VEHICLE AND CERTIFIES THAT AT THE TIME OF DELIVERY THE SAME IS SUBJECT TO THE LIENS OR ENCUMBRANCES NAMED IN THE PURCHASER'S APPLICATION FOR NEW CERTIFICATE OF TITLE AND NONE OTHER.

PURCHASER'S FIRST, MIDDLE AND LAST NAMES (PRINT IN INK OR TYPE)   STREET OR R.F.D.   CITY OR TOWN

(FEDERAL AND STATE REGULATIONS REQUIRE YOU TO STATE THE ODOMETER MILEAGE UPON TRANSFER OF OWNERSHIP (G. S. 20-347).)

I CERTIFY TO THE BEST OF MY KNOWLEDGE THAT THE ODOMETER READING IS [Odometer Reading] AND REFLECTS THE ACTUAL MILEAGE OF THE VEHICLE UNLESS ONE OR MORE OF THE FOLLOWING STATEMENTS IS CHECKED:
- 1. THE AMOUNT OF MILEAGE STATED IS IN EXCESS OF 99,999 MILES OR
- 2. THE ODOMETER READING IS NOT THE ACTUAL MILEAGE AND SHOULD NOT BE RELIED UPON
- 3. THE ODOMETER WAS ALTERED FOR REPAIR OR REPLACEMENT PURPOSES BY

ON _____ AND APPROXIMATELY _____ MILES WERE REMOVED BY THE ALTERATION.

PURCHASER'S SIGNATURE

DATE VEHICLE DELIVERED TO PURCHASER

ALL ANSWERS SUPPLIED AND COMPLETELY SUBSCRIBED AND SWORN TO BEFORE ME THIS ___ DAY OF ___

19 ___

MY COMMISSION EXPIRES: _____

DEALER'S NAME (TO AGREE WITH LICENSE)   DEALER CERTIFICATE NO.

BY: _____

AUTHORIZED AGENT TO SIGN HERE AFTER ENTERING NAME OF PURCHASER   SIGNATURE OF NOTARY PUBLIC IN INK   (SEAL)

A. ALTERATIONS OR ERASURES WILL VOID THIS TITLE
B. LIEN OR ENCUMBRANCE—ENTER IN OWNER'S APPLICATION FOR TITLE
C. RETAIL PURCHASER MUST APPLY FOR NEW TITLE WITHIN 20 DAYS AFTER PURCHASE OR PAY STATUTORY PENALTY

A. Full typed or printed name of purchaser.
B. Purchaser's street address.
C. Purchaser's city or town.
D. Odometer reading on date of re-assignment of title.
E. Purchaser's full signature.
F. Date vehicle delivered to purchaser.
G. Full typed or printed name of dealer.
H. Dealer's certificate number.

I. Signature of dealer's agent (omission of this item will cause application to be rejected).
J. Date notary takes certification.
K. Month notary takes certification.
L. Year notary takes certification.
M. Month, date, and year notary's commission expires.
N. Notary's signature as it appears in the seal or stamp.

Example: Alec Wilder Stewart sells his 2002 BMW to Hawkins Motor Company. Hawkins then sells the BMW to David Rose French. Both transactions take place in Charlotte, North Carolina, before different Mecklenburg County notaries.

A

ASSIGNMENT OF TITLE BY REGISTERED OWNER

FOR VALUE RECEIVED, THE UNDERSIGNED HEREBY SELLS, ASSIGNS OR TRANSFERS THE VEHICLE DESCRIBED ON THE REVERSE SIDE OF THIS CERTIFICATE UNTO THE PURCHASER WHOSE NAME APPEARS IN THIS BLOCK AND HEREBY WARRANTS THE TITLE TO SAID VEHICLE AND CERTIFIES THAT AT THE TIME OF DELIVERY THE SAME IS SUBJECT TO THE LIENS OR ENCUMBRANCES NAMED IN THE PURCHASER'S APPLICATION FOR NEW CERTIFICATE OF TITLE AND NONE OTHER.

Hawkins Motor Company   2 Lions Blvd.   Charlotte

PURCHASER'S FIRST, MIDDLE AND LAST NAMES (PRINT IN INK OR TYPE)   STREET OR R.F.D.   CITY OR TOWN

(FEDERAL AND STATE REGULATIONS REQUIRE YOU TO STATE THE ODOMETER MILEAGE UPON TRANSFER OF OWNERSHIP (G. S. 20-347).)

I CERTIFY TO THE BEST OF MY KNOWLEDGE THAT THE ODOMETER READING IS | **Odometer Reading** | AND REFLECTS THE ACTUAL
MILEAGE OF THE VEHICLE UNLESS ONE OR MORE OF THE FOLLOWING STATEMENTS. | 88049 | IS CHECKED:

- ☐ 1. THE AMOUNT OF MILEAGE STATED IS IN EXCESS OF 99,999 MILES OR
- ☐ 2. THE ODOMETER READING IS NOT THE ACTUAL MILEAGE AND SHOULD NOT BE RELIED UPON.
- ☐ 3. THE ODOMETER WAS ALTERED FOR REPAIR OR REPLACEMENT PURPOSES BY

ON _____ AND APPROXIMATELY _____ MILES WERE REMOVED BY THE ALTERATION.

Hawkins Motor Company by _Jennifer Grayson_

8/19/2004   PURCHASER'S SIGNATURE

DATE VEHICLE DELIVERED TO PURCHASER

Alec Wilder Stewart   ALL ANSWERS SUPPLIED AND COMPLETELY SUBSCRIBED AND SWORN TO BEFORE ME THIS 19th DAY OF August

SELLER'S SIGNATURE   2004

MY COMMISSION EXPIRES: February 5, 2007

Allison Buksterbaum (SEAL)

SIGNATURE OF NOTARY PUBLIC IN INK

B

RE-ASSIGNMENT OF TITLE BY REGISTERED DEALER

FOR VALUE RECEIVED, THE UNDERSIGNED HEREBY SELLS, ASSIGNS OR TRANSFERS THE VEHICLE DESCRIBED ON THE REVERSE SIDE OF THIS CERTIFICATE UNTO THE PURCHASER WHOSE NAME APPEARS IN THIS BLOCK AND HEREBY WARRANTS THE TITLE TO SAID VEHICLE AND CERTIFIES THAT AT THE TIME OF DELIVERY THE SAME IS SUBJECT TO THE LIENS OR ENCUMBRANCES NAMED IN THE PURCHASER'S APPLICATION FOR NEW CERTIFICATE OF TITLE AND NONE OTHER.

David Rose French   4 Talmage Ct.   Charlotte

PURCHASER'S FIRST, MIDDLE AND LAST NAMES (PRINT IN INK OR TYPE)   STREET OR R.F.D.   CITY OR TOWN

(FEDERAL AND STATE REGULATIONS REQUIRE YOU TO STATE THE ODOMETER MILEAGE UPON TRANSFER OF OWNERSHIP (G. S. 20-347).)

I CERTIFY TO THE BEST OF MY KNOWLEDGE THAT THE ODOMETER READING IS | **Odometer Reading** | AND REFLECTS THE ACTUAL
MILEAGE OF THE VEHICLE UNLESS ONE OR MORE OF THE FOLLOWING STATEMENTS. | 88049 | IS CHECKED:

- ☐ 1. THE AMOUNT OF MILEAGE STATED IS IN EXCESS OF 99,999 MILES OR
- ☐ 2. THE ODOMETER READING IS NOT THE ACTUAL MILEAGE AND SHOULD NOT BE RELIED UPON.
- ☐ 3. THE ODOMETER WAS ALTERED FOR REPAIR OR REPLACEMENT PURPOSES BY

ON _____ AND APPROXIMATELY _____ MILES WERE REMOVED BY THE ALTERATION.

David Rose French

PURCHASER'S SIGNATURE

8/20/2004

DATE VEHICLE DELIVERED TO PURCHASER

ALL ANSWERS SUPPLIED AND COMPLETELY SUBSCRIBED AND SWORN TO BEFORE ME THIS 20th DAY OF August

2004

Hawkins Motor Company 8116

DEALER'S NAME (TO AGREE WITH LICENSE)   DEALER CERTIFICATE NO.

MY COMMISSION EXPIRES: 3/31/2007

BY _Rose Xavier Stephens_   _Mary Jass Stewart_ (SEAL)

AUTHORIZED AGENT TO SIGN HERE AFTER ENTERING NAME OF PURCHASER   SIGNATURE OF NOTARY PUBLIC IN INK

A. ALTERATIONS OR ERASURES WILL VOID THIS TITLE

B. LIEN OR ENCUMBRANCE—ENTER IN OWNER'S APPLICATION FOR TITLE

C. RETAIL PURCHASER MUST APPLY FOR NEW TITLE WITHIN 20 DAYS AFTER PURCHASE OR PAY STATUTORY PENALTY

Form V—The MVR-1

Form V is the latest version of the application-for-title form (MVR-1) that must be used when the former owner has assigned his or her title by means of a DMV certificate of title form that does not contain a section for the purchaser to apply for a new certificate of title (Form IV, for example). The MVR-1 is rather complicated, and if the person who appears before the notary to certify execution of the application has difficulty completing the form or has questions about it, the notary should refer him or her to the nearest motor vehicle registration office (the notary should do this any time a person has difficulty completing a title document). The notary is concerned only with the owner/applicant's signature and the acknowledgment.

MVR-1
(Rev. 8/99)

North Carolina Division of Motor Vehicles

TITLE APPLICATION

VEHICLE SECTION

YEAR	MAKE	BODY STYLE	SERIES MODEL	VEHICLE IDENTIFICATION NUMBER	FUEL TYPE

OWNER SECTION

Owner 1 ID # _____

Full Legal Name of Owner 1 (First, Middle, Last, Suffix) or Company Name

Owner 2 ID # _____

Full Legal Name of Owner 2 (First, Middle, Last, Suffix) or Company Name

Residence Address (Individual) Business Address (Firm)

City and State		Zip Code	Tax County

Mail Address (if different from above)

LIEN SECTION

FIRST LIEN		SECOND LIEN	
Date of Lien	ACCOUNT #	Date of Lien	ACCOUNT #
Lienholder ID#	Lienholder Name	Lienholder ID#	Lienholder Name

Address _____   Address _____

City _____ State _____ Zip Code _____   City _____ State _____ Zip Code _____

CHECK Appropriate Block/s

ODOMETER READING

☐ Title Only -- Vehicle Not in Operation   ☐ Exchanged Plate No. _____

☐ Title and License
   Class of License _____   ☐ Replaced Plate No. _____

☐ Plate No. Transferred _____   ☐ Truck Weight desired _____

Expiration Date _____

I certify for the motor vehicle described above that I have financial responsibility as required by law.

Insurance company authorized in N.C.   Policy Number

Date First Operated in N.C.	State of Last Registration	Passenger Capacity	N.C. Dealer No.	Empty Weight	Combined Gross Weight of Truck or Truck-Tractor with Trailer

Purchased		Purchased for Use in N.C.	From Whom Purchased (Name and address)	Purchase Date
☐ New	☐ Used	☐ Yes ☐ No		

Is This Vehicle Leased? ☐ Yes ☐ No	SALES PRICE
If Yes, Attach Form 330 or Lease Agreement Equipment #	

DISCLOSURE SECTION

All motor vehicle records maintained by the North Carolina Division of Motor Vehicles will remain closed for marketing and solicitation unless the block below is checked.

☐ I (We) would like the personal information contained in this application **to be available for disclosure.**

APPLICATION MUST BE SIGNED IN INK BY EACH OWNER OR AUTHORIZED REPRESENTATIVE OF FIRMS OR CORPORATIONS.

I (we) am (are) the owner(s) of the vehicle described on this application and request that a North Carolina Certificate of Title be issued. I (we) certify that the information on the application is correct to the best of my (our) knowledge. The vehicle is subject to the liens named and no others. If a registration plate is issued or transferred, I (we) further certify that there has not been a registration plate revocation and that liability insurance is in effect on this vehicle on the date of this application as required by the North Carolina Financial Security Act of 1957.

OWNER'S SIGNATURE _____

Acknowledged before me this _____ day of _____ My commission expires _____

(SEAL)   Notary Public _____

Example (continuing the example from Form IV): When David Rose French applies for a title to the 2002 BMW in his name, he will use Form V. When he appears before a notary to acknowledge execution of the application, it will be taken as follows:

☐ Plate No. Transferred _____		☐ Truck Weight desired _____			
Expiration Date _____					

I certify for the motor vehicle described above that I have financial responsibility as required by law.

State First Insurance _____   45845554544

Insurance company authorized in N.C.   Policy Number

Date First Operated in N.C.	State of Last Registration	Passenger Capacity	N.C. Dealer No.	Empty Weight	Combined Gross Weight of Truck or Truck-Tractor with Trailer
8-20-2004	NC	4	8116	4550	

Purchased	Purchased for Use in N.C.	From Whom Purchased (Name and address)	Purchase Date
☐ New ☒ Used	☒ Yes ☐ No	HAWKINS MOTOR CO.	8-20-2004

Is This Vehicle Leased? ☐ Yes ☒ No		SALES PRICE
If Yes, Attach Form 330 or Lease Agreement	Equipment #	21,985

DISCLOSURE SECTION

All motor vehicle records maintained by the North Carolina Division of Motor Vehicles will remain closed for marketing and solicitation unless the block below is checked.

   ☐ I (We) would like the personal information contained in this application **to be available for disclosure.**

APPLICATION MUST BE SIGNED IN INK BY EACH OWNER OR AUTHORIZED REPRESENTATIVE OF FIRMS OR CORPORATIONS.

I (we) am (are) the owner(s) of the vehicle described on this application and request that a North Carolina Certificate of Title be issued. I (we) certify that the information on the application is correct to the best of my (our) knowledge. The vehicle is subject to the liens named and no others. If a registration plate is issued or transferred, I (we) further certify that there has not been a registration plate revocation and that liability insurance is in effect on this vehicle on the date of this application as required by the North Carolina Financial Security Act of 1957.

OWNER'S SIGNATURE   *David Rose French* _____

Acknowledged before me this 20th day of August, 2004   My commission expires   10-21-2008

    (SEAL)   Notary Public   *David Knox*

V

OATHS

Whenever the notarial certificate contains the words "sworn to" or "duly sworn," the notary public must administer an oath to the person whose acknowledgment or proof is being taken. Throughout this chapter, the word "oath" should be understood to include "affirmation," which is a solemn pledge or declaration and may be used in place of an oath by any person who prefers not to take an oath (affirmations are discussed further under "Procedure" below). A notary should *always* administer an oath when the attestation certificate calls for one.

Notary's Authority

Under North Carolina law, a notary public may administer any oath, including an oath of office, except when the law requires that another official administer the particular oath.[1] For example, a notary may not administer the oath of office to another notary, because a statute specifically provides that notaries must take this oath before a register of deeds.[2] Whenever the law prescribes an oath without specifying the officer before whom it must be taken, a notary may administer the oath.

Under federal law, a North Carolina notary acting within North Carolina may administer any oath authorized or required under the laws of the United States,[3] including oaths of office for all federal offices.[4] In addition to this general authorization, notaries are specifically authorized to take oaths of office for national-bank directors[5] and oaths with respect to adverse claims of mining rights.[6]

---

1. N.C. GEN. STAT. §§ 10A-9(a)(2) and 11-7.1(a)(3) (hereinafter G.S.).
2. G.S. 10A-8.
3. 5 U.S.C. § 2903(c)(2).
4. 5 U.S.C. § 2903(a).
5. 12 U.S.C. § 73.
6. 30 U.S.C. § 31.

Procedure

A person taking an oath should place one hand on the Holy Scriptures.[7] This book will vary depending on the person's religious beliefs: Christians should use the New Testament or the Bible; Jews, the Torah or the Old Testament; Moslems, the Koran; Hindus, the Bhagavad-Gita; and so forth.

A person who affirms rather than swears should use the same words as the oath, except that he or she should say "affirm" rather than "swear" and should omit the words "so help me, God."[8] A person being affirmed is not required to place his or her hand on any book or document.

All oaths of office and many other oaths must be subscribed by the person who gives the oath and then filed in a particular place.[9] If the oath does not appear on a printed form, the proper procedure is to type out the text, administer it to the person, have him or her sign it, and attest it in the following fashion:[10]

Sworn to and subscribed before me this _____ day of _____, 20___.
(Official Seal)   _____
Notary Public
My commission expires _____, 20___.

The person being sworn is responsible for filing the subscribed and attested oath in the proper office.

Oaths of Office

All persons elected or appointed to public office in this state must take an oath to support the constitutions of the United States and North Carolina. The constitutional oath is as follows:

> I, _____, do solemnly swear [or affirm] that I will support and maintain the Constitution and laws of the United States, and the Constitution and laws of North Carolina not inconsistent therewith, and that I will faithfully discharge the duties of my office as _____, so help me, God. [11]

---

7. G.S. 11-2.
8. G.S. 11-4.
9. *See, e.g.,* G.S. 14-229.
10. This form of acknowledgment is known as a *jurat.*
11. N.C. CONST. art. VI, § 7.

Oaths of Corporations

The oath of a corporation is given by and through an officer or agent of the corporation authorized by law to verify pleadings on behalf of the corporation.[12] The interested parties are responsible for seeing that the appropriate officer appears before the notary to take an oath for a corporation.

---

12. G.S. 11-5.

VI

AFFIDAVITS

An affidavit is a voluntary statement in writing sworn to or affirmed as true before an officer authorized to administer oaths.[1] The purpose of an affidavit is "to obtain the sworn statement of facts . . . of the affiant [the person making the affidavit] in such official and authoritative shape, as that it may be used for any lawful purposes, either in or out of courts of justice."[2] Unlike depositions, which are usually compelled and taken only after notice to all parties to a lawsuit, affidavits are voluntary statements used in a wide variety of governmental and business affairs—as evidence of, for example, a person's age, the title to property, the pedigree of animals, and the financial condition of a loan applicant.

Notary's Authority

A North Carolina notary public acting within North Carolina may take affidavits[3] except when the law prescribes another official before whom a specific affidavit must be sworn. For example, a statute provides that only the clerk of superior court can take an insolvent debtor's affidavit for assignment of his or her estate for the benefit of creditors.[4] Also, a notary may not take his or her own affidavit, since a notary may not administer an oath to him- or herself.[5]

Like North Carolina law, federal law allows affidavits to be used in many ways. Because a North Carolina notary acting within North Carolina may administer oaths under federal law,[6] he or she may also take affidavits under federal law except for specific affidavits that must be taken by another designated official.

---

1. BLACK'S LAW DICTIONARY 80 (4th ed. 1951).
2. Alford v. McCormac, 90 N.C. 151, 153 (1884).
3. N.C. GEN. STAT. § 10A-9(a)(2) (hereinafter G.S.).
4. G.S. 23-13.
5. G.S. 10A-9(c)(1).
6. 5 U.S.C. § 2903(c)(2).

Components

An affidavit has the following components:

Caption. An affidavit for a legal proceeding should include a caption that recites the county and state in which the action is pending, the names of the parties, the name of the court, and the label "Affidavit." Other affidavits should include a title briefly describing the nature of the matter and naming the county and state in which the affidavit was given.

Preamble. The preamble follows the caption and is simply a statement that the named person appeared before the notary, was duly sworn, and made the following affidavit. Although not essential to an affidavit's validity, the preamble is usually included for introductory purposes.

Allegations. The statements of the affiant follow the preamble, usually in numbered paragraphs, each paragraph containing only one allegation. The first allegation should always state the affiant's relationship to the action or to the parties.

Affiant's signature. Although the absence of this signature does not technically invalidate an affidavit,[7] the affiant should sign his or her name below the allegations. Omission of a signature raises doubts about the affidavit's validity and may invalidate it in other states.

Jurat. The jurat, or notary's certificate that the affidavit was subscribed and sworn to (or affirmed) at a specified time and place, appears after the affiant's signature. The jurat should be attested by a notary in the usual manner.

Procedure

Although a statement may be reduced to writing in a notary's presence when it is sworn to or affirmed, it is usually already in writing when brought before the notary. In either case, the notary should administer the following oath according to the procedure described in Chapter V:

> Do you swear [or affirm] that the statements contained in this writing are the truth, by your own knowledge or by your information and belief, so help you, God?

After taking the oath, the affiant signs the affidavit or identifies an earlier signature as his or her own, and the notary adds his or her certificate (jurat) and attestation. "Subscribed and sworn to [or affirmed] before me this _____ day of _____, 20___" is sufficient.

---

7. *Alford*, 90 N.C. 151.

Preparing an affidavit sufficient to accomplish the desired result is the responsibility of the party and the party's attorney. The notary's duties are, first, to ensure that the affiant is who he or she claims to be (persons not known to the notary should be asked to identify themselves appropriately) and swears to the truthfulness of the statements in the affidavit, and, second, to certify the affidavit properly.

Verification of Pleadings

In some kinds of lawsuits—such as divorce,[8] habeas corpus,[9] or certain suits by shareholders or members of a corporation or unincorporated association[10]—the parties or their attorneys must verify the pleadings (complaints filed by the plaintiff and answers filed by the defendant); this is done by executing an affidavit of verification according to Rule 11 of the North Carolina Rules of Civil Procedure. The content of the affidavit varies according to the type of lawsuit, and the party seeking the affidavit and his or her attorney are responsible for preparing it correctly. The notary's responsibilities are to administer an oath and to complete the jurat, or certification, correctly.

Forms

The two basic forms for affidavits—one for private matters, the other for legal proceedings—are below. Sample affidavits are available from many sources. Some may be found in *Douglas' Forms* (5th ed. 1998), published by Hunton & Williams; Archibald Scales III; and Smith Debnam Narron Wyche Story & Myers, LLP. Some are also available in C. Farber, *2004–2005 U.S. Notary Reference Manual: A Guide to Notarization Requirements for All U.S. States and Jurisdictions*, published and updated annually by the National Notary Association.

Private matters

The following form is the general affidavit for use between private parties, not in legal proceedings. The components of an affidavit (discussed above) are indicated by marginal notes.

---

8. G.S. 50-8.
9. G.S. 17-7(5).
10. N.C. R. Civ. P. 23(b).

[Caption or title]

North Carolina

Affidavit

_____ County

[Preamble]

_____, appearing before the undersigned notary and being duly sworn, says that:

[Allegations]
Set out title or position, residence, and relationship to the parties or the matter for which the affidavit is desired.

Set out declarations of affiant in numbered paragraphs.

1. He (or she) is_____

_____

_____

_____

_____

2. _____

_____

_____

_____

[Affiant's signature]

_____

Affiant

Sworn to (or affirmed) and subscribed before me this _____ day of _____, 20___.

[Jurat]

(Official Seal)

_____

Notary Public

My commission expires _____, 20___.

Note: The following preamble may be used instead of the one above:

_____ personally appeared
before me in _____,
_____ County, State of
_____, and having been duly sworn
(or affirmed), according to law, made the following affidavit,
to wit: . . . .

Legal proceedings

The following is the usual form of an affidavit for a court or other legal proceeding. The components of such an affidavit (discussed above) are indicated by marginal notes.

[Venue]

North Carolina

General Court of Justice

_____ Court Division

_____ County

_____

Plaintiff(s)

[Caption or title]

vs.   Affidavit

_____

Defendant(s)

[Preamble]

_____, appearing before the undersigned notary and being duly sworn, says that:

[Allegations]

Set out title or position, residence, and relationship to the parties or the matter for which the affidavit is desired.

1. He (or she) is_____

_____

_____

_____

_____

_____

Set out declarations of affiant in numbered paragraphs.

2. _____

_____

_____

[Affiant's signature]

_____

Affiant

Sworn to (or affirmed) and subscribed before me this _____ day of _____, 20___.

[Jurat]

(Official Seal)

_____

Notary Public

My commission expires _____, 20___.

VII

RESOURCES FOR NOTARIES

A basic resource for notaries in North Carolina is the Web site maintained by The Notary Public Section of the North Carolina Department of the Secretary of State: www.sosnc.com or www.secretary.state.nc.us/notary. On this site, you can see a list of frequently asked questions, find example forms, and get information about changes in the law concerning notaries. The National Notary Association also has a helpful Web site: www.nationalnotary.org.

Additional printed resources that may be useful include:

- *Anderson's Manual for Notaries Public.* Ninth edition by The Publisher's Staff. Anderson Publishing Co., 2001.

- *Notary Law & Practice: Cases & Materials.* By Michael L. Closen, Glen-Peter Ahlers, Robert M. Jarvis, Malcom L. Morris, and Nancy P. Spyke. National Notary Association, 1997.

- *2004–2005 U.S. Notary Reference Manual: A Guide to Notarization Requirements for All U.S. States and Jurisdictions.* Charles N. Farber. National Notary Association. Updated annually.

Appendix I contains North Carolina General Statutes Chapter 10A, Notaries. Readers should also check up-to-date statutory sources for changes in these statutes. Appendix II provides a chart listing statutory requirements notaries must follow in cases of name, residence, or other status changes. Appendix III contains a glossary of terms that a notary may encounter. Finally, Appendix IV contains frequently asked questions and answers, provided by The Notary Public Section of the North Carolina Department of the Secretary of State.

Appendix I

Text of General Statutes
(current through August 17, 2004)

CHAPTER 10A. NOTARIES

§ 10A-1. Short title.
This act is the Notary Public Act and may be cited by that name.

§ 10A-2. Purposes.
This Chapter shall be construed and applied to advance its underlying purposes, which are:
(1) To promote, serve, and protect the public interests.
(2) To simplify, clarify, and modernize the law governing notaries.
(3) To prevent fraud and forgery.

§ 10A-3. Definitions.
The following definitions apply in this Chapter:
(1) Acknowledgment.—A notarial act in which a notary certifies that a signer, whose identity is personally known to the notary or proven on the basis of satisfactory evidence, has admitted, in the notary's presence, having signed a document voluntarily.
(2) Commission.—The written authority to perform a notarial act.
(2a) Director.—The Director of the Notary Section of the Department of the Secretary of State.
(3) Notarial act, notary act, and notarization.—Any act that a notary is empowered to perform under G.S. 10A-9.
(4) Notary public and notary.—A person commissioned to perform notarial acts under this Chapter.
(5) Oath or affirmation.—A notarial act in which a notary certifies that a person made a vow or affirmation in the presence of the notary, with reference made to a Supreme Being for an oath and with no reference made to a Supreme Being for an affirmation.

(6)   Official misconduct.—Either of the following:

a. A notary's performance of a prohibited act or failure to perform a mandated act set forth in this Chapter or any other law in connection with notarization.

b. A notary's performance of a notarial act in a manner found by the Secretary to be negligent or against the public interest.

(7)   Personal knowledge of identity.—Familiarity with an individual resulting from interactions with that individual over a period of time sufficient to eliminate every reasonable doubt that the individual has the identity claimed.

(8)   Satisfactory evidence of identity.—Identification of an individual based on either of the following:

a. One current document issued by a federal or state government with the individual's photograph.

b. Identification by a credible person who is personally known to the notary and who has personal knowledge of the individual's identity.

(8a)   Secretary.—The Secretary of State.

(9)   Verification or proof.—A notarial act in which a notary certifies that a signer, whose identity is personally known to the notary or proven on the basis of satisfactory evidence, has, in the notary's presence, voluntarily signed a document and taken an oath or affirmation concerning the document.

§ 10A-4. Commissioning.

(a) Except as provided in subsection (c) of this section, the Secretary shall commission as a notary any qualified person who submits an application in accordance with this Chapter.

(b) A person qualified for a notarial commission shall meet all of the following requirements:

(1)   Be at least 18 years of age.

(2)   Reside or work in this State.

(3)   Satisfactorily complete a course of study that is approved by the Secretary and consists of not less than three hours nor more than six hours of classroom instruction provided by community colleges throughout the State, unless the person is a licensed member of the Bar of this State.

(4)   Purchase and keep as a reference a manual approved by the Secretary that describes the duties, authority, and ethical responsibilities of notaries public.

(5)   Submit an application containing no significant misstatement or omission of fact. The application form shall be provided by the Secretary and be available at the register of deeds office in each county. Every application shall bear the signature of the applicant written with pen and ink, and the signature shall be acknowledged by the applicant

before a person authorized to administer oaths. The applicant shall also obtain the recommendation of one publicly elected official in North Carolina whose recommendation shall be contained on the application.

(6)　Pay a nonrefundable fee of fifty dollars ($50.00).

(c) The Secretary may deny an application for commission or recommission as a notary if any of the following applies to the applicant:

(1)　The applicant has been convicted of a crime involving dishonesty or moral turpitude.

(1a)　The applicant has been convicted of a felony and the applicant's rights have not been restored.

(2)　The applicant has had a notarial commission or professional license revoked, suspended, or restricted by this or any other state.

(3)　The applicant has engaged in official misconduct, whether or not disciplinary action resulted.

(4)　The applicant knowingly uses false or misleading advertising in which the applicant as a notary represents that the applicant has powers, duties, rights or privileges that the applicant does not possess by law.

(5)　The applicant is found by a court of this State or any other state to have engaged in the unauthorized practice of law.

§ 10A-5. Length of term and jurisdiction.

A person commissioned under this Chapter may perform notarial acts in any part of this State for a term of five years, unless the commission is revoked under G.S. 10A-13(d) or resigned under G.S. 10A-13(c).

§ 10A-6. Recommissioning.

An applicant for recommissioning as a notary shall submit a new application and comply anew with the provisions of G.S. 10A-4, except that the applicant shall not be required to complete the course of study described in subdivision (b)(3) nor to obtain the recommendation of a publicly elected official.

§ 10A-7. Instructor's certification.

(a) The course of study required by G.S. 10A-4(b) shall be taught by an instructor certified in accordance with rules adopted by the Secretary. An instructor must meet the following requirements to be certified to teach a course of study for notaries public:

(1)　Complete and pass a six-hour instructor's course taught by the Director or other person approved by the Secretary.

(2)　Have six months of active experience as a notary public.

(3)　Maintain a current commission as a notary public.

(4)　Purchase the current notary public guidebook.

(5)　Pay a nonrefundable fee of fifty dollars ($50.00).

(b) Certification to teach a course of study for notaries public shall be effective for two years. A certification may be renewed by passing a recertification course taught by the Director or other person approved by the Secretary and by paying a nonrefundable fee of fifty dollars ($50.00).

(c) The following people may be certified to teach a course of study for notaries public without meeting the requirements of subdivisions (a)(2), (a)(3), and (a)(5) of this section, and they may renew their certification without paying the renewal fee, so long as they remain actively employed in the capacities named:

(1)   Registers of deeds.

(2)   Clerks of court.

(3)   The Director.

§ 10A-8. Oath of office.

If granted, a commission shall be sent to the register of deeds of the county where the appointee lives or works and a copy of the letter of transmittal sent to the appointee. The appointee shall appear before the register of deeds to which the commission was delivered within 90 days of commissioning and shall be duly qualified by taking the general oath of office prescribed in G.S. 11-11 and the oath prescribed for officers in G.S. 11-7. The notary shall then place the appointee's signature in a book designated as "The Record of Notaries Public." This Record shall contain the name and signature of the notary, the effective date and expiration date of the commission, the date the oath was administered, and the date of any revocation or resignation. The Record shall constitute the official record of the qualification of notaries public. The register of deeds shall deliver the commission to the notary following completion of the requirements of this section and shall notify the Secretary of State of the delivery.

If the appointee does not appear before the register of deeds within 90 days, the appointee must reapply for commissioning and the register of deeds must return the commission to the Secretary of State. If the appointee reapplies within one year of the granting of the commission, the Secretary of State may waive the requirements of subdivisions G.S. 10A-4(b)(3) and (4).

§ 10A-9. Powers and limitations.

(a) A notary may perform any of the following notarial acts:

(1)   Acknowledgments.

(2)   Oaths and affirmations.

(3)   Verifications or proofs.

(b) A notarial act shall be attested by all of the following:

(1)   The signature of the notary, exactly as shown on the notary's commission.

(2)   The readable appearance of the notary's name, either from the notary's signature or from the notary's typed, printed, or embossed name near the signature.

(3)   The clear and legible appearance of the notary's stamp or seal.

(4)   A statement of the date the notary's commission expires.

(c) A notary is disqualified from performing a notarial act if any of the following apply:

(1)   The notary is a signer of or is named, other than as a trustee in a deed of trust, in the document that is to be notarized.

(2)   The notary will receive directly from a transaction connected with the notarial act any commission, fee, advantage, right, title, interest, cash, property, or other consideration exceeding in value the fees specified in G.S. 10A-10, other than fees or other consideration paid for services rendered by a licensed attorney, a licensed real estate broker or salesperson, a motor vehicle dealer, or a banker.

(d) A notarial act performed in another jurisdiction by a notary public of that jurisdiction is valid to the same extent as if it had been performed by a notary commissioned under this Chapter.

(e) Commissioned officers on active duty in the United States armed forces who are authorized under 10 U.S.C. § 936 to perform notarial acts may perform the acts for persons serving in or with the United States armed forces, their spouses, and their dependents.

(f) The Secretary of State and register of deeds in the county in which a notary qualified may certify to the commission of the notary.

(g) A notary public who is not an attorney licensed to practice law in this State who advertises the person's services as a notary public in a language other than English, by radio, television, signs, pamphlets, newspapers, other written communication, or in any other manner, shall post or otherwise include with the advertisement the notice set forth in this subsection in English and in the language used for the advertisement. The notice shall be of conspicuous size, if in writing, and shall state: "I AM NOT AN ATTORNEY LICENSED TO PRACTICE LAW IN THE STATE OF NORTH CAROLINA, AND I MAY NOT GIVE LEGAL ADVICE OR ACCEPT FEES FOR LEGAL ADVICE." If the advertisement is by radio or television, the statement may be modified but must include substantially the same message.

(h) A notary public who is not an attorney licensed to practice law in this State is prohibited from representing or advertising that the notary public is an "immigration consultant" or expert on immigration matters unless the notary public is an accredited representative of an organization recognized by the Board of Immigration Appeals pursuant to Title 8, Part 292, Section 2(a–e) of the Code of Federal Regulations (8 CFR 292.2(a–e)).

(i) A notary public who is not an attorney licensed to practice law in this State is prohibited from rendering any service that constitutes the unauthorized practice of law.

(j) A notary public required to comply with the provisions of subsection (g) of this section shall prominently post at the notary public's place of business a schedule of fees established by law, which a notary public may charge. The fee schedule shall be written in English and in the non-English language in which the notary services were solicited, and shall contain the notice required in subsection (g) of this section, unless the notice is otherwise prominently posted at the notary public's place of business.

§ 10A-10. Fees of notaries.

The maximum fees that may be charged by a notary for notarial acts are as follows:

(1) For acknowledgments, three dollars ($3.00) per signature.

(2) For oaths or affirmations without a verification or proof, three dollars ($3.00) per person.

(3) For verifications or proofs, three dollars ($3.00) per signature.

§ 10A-11. Notarial stamp or seal.

A notary public shall provide and keep an official stamp or seal. The stamp or seal shall clearly show and legibly reproduce under photographic methods, when embossed, stamped, impressed, or affixed to a document, the name of the notary exactly as it appears on the commission, the name of the county in which appointed and qualified, the words "North Carolina" or an abbreviation thereof, and the words "Notary Public". The official stamp or seal, as it appears on a document, may contain a permanently imprinted or a handwritten expiration date of the notary's commission. A notary public shall replace a seal that has become so worn that it can no longer clearly show or legibly reproduce under photographic methods the information required by this section. The stamp or seal is the property and responsibility of the notary whose name appears on it. However, upon revocation, the notary shall immediately surrender the stamp or seal to the Secretary.

§ 10A-12. Enforcement and penalties.

(a) Any person who holds himself or herself out to the public as a notary or who performs notarial acts and is not commissioned is guilty of a Class 1 misdemeanor.

(b) Any notary who takes an acknowledgment or performs a verification or proof without personal knowledge of the signer's identity or without satisfactory evidence of the signer's identity is guilty of a Class 2 misdemeanor.

(c) Any notary who takes an acknowledgment or performs a verification or proof knowing it is false or fraudulent is guilty of a Class I felony.

(d) Any person who knowingly solicits or coerces a notary to commit official misconduct is guilty of a Class 1 misdemeanor.

(e) For purposes of enforcing this Chapter, the law enforcement agents of the Department of the Secretary of State have statewide jurisdiction and have all of the powers and authority of law enforcement officers when executing arrest warrants. The agents have the authority to assist local law enforcement agencies in their investigations and to initiate and carry out, on their own or in coordination with local law enforcement agencies, investigations of violations of this Chapter.

(f) The Secretary of State, through the Attorney General, may seek injunctive relief against any notary public who violates the provisions of this Chapter. Nothing in this Chapter diminishes the authority of the North Carolina State Bar.

(g) A violation of G.S. 10A-9(h) or (i) constitutes a deceptive trade practice under G.S. 75-1.1.

§ 10A-13. Change of status.

(a) Within 30 days after the change of a notary's residence address, the notary shall notify the Secretary of State, by certified or registered mail, and provide a signed notice of the change, giving both the old and new addresses.

(b) Within 30 days after changing names, a notary shall notify the Secretary of State of the change by submitting a new application. The Secretary of State shall cancel the notary's commission under the old name, issue a commission under the new name, direct the notary to reappear before the register of deeds to take the oath of office, and direct the register of deeds to correct The Record of Notaries Public.

(c) A notary who resigns a commission shall deliver to the Secretary of State, by certified or registered mail, a notice indicating the effective date of resignation. Notaries who neither reside nor work in the State shall resign their commission.

(d) The Secretary of State may revoke a notarial commission on any ground for which an application for a commission may be denied under G.S. 10A-4(c). The Secretary of State may revoke the commission of a notary who fails to administer an oath or affirmation when performing a notarial act that requires the administering of an oath or affirmation.

§ 10A-14. Notaries ex officio.

(a) The clerks of the superior court may act as notaries public in their several counties by virtue of their offices as clerks and may certify their notarial acts only under the seals of their respective courts. Assistant and deputy clerks of superior court, by virtue of their offices, may perform the following notarial acts and may certify these notarial acts only under the seals of their respective courts:

(1) Oaths and affirmations.
(2) Verifications or proofs.

Upon completion of the course of study provided for in G.S. 10A-4(b), assistant and deputy clerks of superior court may, by virtue of their offices, perform all other notarial acts and may certify these notarial acts only under the seals of their respective courts. A course of study attended only by assistant and deputy clerks of superior court may be taught at any mutually convenient location agreed to by the Secretary and the Administrative Officer of the Courts.

(b) Registers of deeds may act as notaries public in their several counties by virtue of their offices as registers of deeds and may certify their notarial acts only under the seals of their respective offices. Assistant and deputy registers of deeds, by virtue of their offices, may perform the following notarial acts and may certify these notarial acts only under the seals of their respective offices:

(1)   Oaths and affirmations.

(2)   Verifications or proofs.

Upon completion of the course of study provided for in G.S. 10A-4(b), assistant and deputy registers of deeds may, by virtue of their offices, perform all other notarial acts and may certify these notarial acts only under the seals of their respective offices. A course of study attended only by assistant and deputy registers of deeds may be taught at any mutually convenient location agreed to by the Secretary and the North Carolina Association of Registers of Deeds.

(c) The Director may act as a notary public by virtue of the Director's employment in the Department of the Secretary of State and may certify a notarial act performed in that capacity under the seal of the Secretary of State.

(d) Unless otherwise provided by law, a person designated a notary public by this section may charge a fee for a notarial act performed in accordance with G.S. 10A-10. The fee authorized by this section is payable to the governmental unit or agency by whom the person is employed.

(e) Nothing in this section shall authorize a person to act as a notary public other than in the performance of the official duties of the person's office unless the person complies fully with the requirements of G.S. 10A-4.

§ 10A-15. Repealed.

§ 10A-16. Acts of notaries public in certain instances validated.

(a) Any acknowledgment taken and any instrument notarized by a person prior to qualification as a notary public but after commissioning or recommissioning as a notary public, or by a person whose notary commission has expired, is hereby validated. The acknowledgment and instrument shall have the same legal effect as if the person qualified as a notary public at the time the person performed the act.

(b) All documents bearing a notarial seal and which contain any of the following errors are validated and given the same legal effect as if the errors had not occurred:

(1)   The date of the expiration of the notary's commission is stated, whether correctly or erroneously.

(2)   The notarial seal does not contain a readable impression of the notary's name, contains an incorrect spelling of the notary's name, or does not bear the name of the notary exactly as it appears on the commission, as required by G.S. 10A-11.

(3)   The notary's signature does not comport exactly with the name on the notary commission or on the notary seal, as required by G.S. 10A-9.

(4)   The notarial seal contains typed, printed, drawn, or handwritten material added to the seal, fails to contain the words "North Carolina" or the abbreviation "N. C.", or contains correct information except that instead of the abbreviation for North Carolina contains the abbreviation for another state.

(c) All deeds of trust in which the notary was named in the document as a trustee only are validated.

(d) This section applies to notarial acts performed on or before February 1, 2004.

§ 10A-17. Certain notarial acts validated.

(a) Any acknowledgment taken and any instrument notarized by a person whose notarial commission was revoked on or before January 30, 1997, is hereby validated.

(b) This section applies to notarial acts performed on or before August 1, 1998.

Appendix II

Requirements Pertaining to Change in the Status of a Notary Public

Change	Requirements	Fee	Oath?	Time frame
Name change	Complete name/ address change form*	None	Yes	Within 30 days of name change
Address change **not** involving a county change	Complete name/ address change form	None	No	Within 30 days of address change
Name and address change **not** involving a county change	Complete name/ address change form*	None	Yes	Within 30 days of name/address change
Name and address change which involves a county change	Complete reappointment form*	$50.00	Yes	Within 30 days of name/address change
County change	Complete reappointment form*	$50.00	Yes	Upon the expiration date of current commission
Lapse of commission for 5 years or more	Complete initial application and take notary public course (Notary Public Section recommendation)	$50.00	Yes	
Change of residence to another state or employment to a business or company outside of N.C.	Submit resignation letter and seal to The Notary Public Section	NA	NA	Immediately

* New seal or stamp required to reflect name and/or county change.

Information provided by The Notary Public Section of the N.C. Department of the Secretary of State, March 2004.

Appendix III

Notary Public Glossary

acknowledgment. A notarial act in which a notary certifies that a signer, whose identity is personally known to the notary or proven on the basis of satisfactory evidence, has admitted, in the notary's presence, having signed a document voluntarily.

acknowledgment, certificate of. A written statement, affixed to a document, signed and sealed by a notary stating in a form that the notary took the acknowledgment of the person who signed the document.

acknowledgment, certificate of (corporate form). A notary's certificate stating that the individual who signed the document was a titled officer of the corporation.

acknowledgment, certificate of (individual form). A notary's certificate stating that a document was signed by a person (individual).

adjudication. A judicial decision, sentence, or decree.

administrator. A party chosen by the court to handle a person's estate. One who manages or oversees.

advocate. (1) To support or argue in favor of a cause. (2) An attorney-at-law.

affiant. The person who takes an oath or affirmation.

affidavit. A document that contains a statement made under oath or affirmation, is signed by the affiant, and includes a jurat signed and sealed by a notary.

affirmation. A solemn statement, equivalent by law to an oath but having no religious significance or reference to a Supreme Being. "Do you solemnly, sincerely, and truly declare and affirm that the statements made by you are true and correct?"

agreement. An understanding, often put in writing and signed, between two or more people.

amendment. A change, correction, or alteration.

apostille. Authentication attached to a notarized and county-certified document created for possible international use.

appeal. Action by a defeated party in a lawsuit to have a judgment reversed.

appointment. (1) A document in which a superior officer designates and/or confers title, powers, responsibility, and authority to another. (2) A notarial appointment.

attest. To indicate genuineness by signing as a witness.

authentic. Genuine, not counterfeit.

authentication. Certification of the genuineness of an official's signature, seal, or position within the State of North Carolina so that the document can be recognized in a foreign jurisdiction.

certificate. A written statement signed by an official, describing acts performed in his or her official capacity.

commission. Authorization granted by the appropriate state authority to exercise the functions and duties of a notary.

conviction. The judicial act of finding a person guilty of a criminal charge.

counterfeit. To make an imitation or copy for the purpose of illegal misrepresentation. A forgery.

countersignature. The signature of a person with an official title necessary to authenticate or validate a document.

crime. A misdemeanor or a felony. A violation of the law that is punishable upon conviction by fine or imprisonment.

deponent. One who makes oath to a written statement. Technically, a person subscribing a deposition but used interchangeably with **affiant.**

deposition. A witness's testimony, which is taken out of court or other hearing or proceeding, under oath or by affirmation before a notary public or other person, officer, or commissioner before whom such testimony is authorized by law to be taken, and which will be used at a trial or hearing.

defraud. To unlawfully trick or deceive.

Director. The Director of the Certification and Filing Division of the N.C. Department of the Secretary of State.

felony. (1) A crime punishable by death or imprisonment in a state prison. (2) A crime defined by statute as a felony.

jurat. Latin for "to swear." A jurat is that part of an affidavit in which the officer (notary public) certifies that the affidavit was sworn to before him or her.

misdemeanor. Any crime other than a felony. Felonies are more serious offenses than misdemeanors.

moral integrity. Conditions or qualities of character and reputation considered necessary for an individual to competently perform specified acts or hold office.

moral turpitude. Conditions or qualities of character or actions that are considered vile, base, wrong, immoral, or improper.

notarization. An act performed in conformance with the notary law (N.C. General Statute 10A-9) by a qualified and commissioned notary public.

notary public. Also called a notary. A person appointed by a state official to serve the public as a disinterested witness, to take acknowledgments, to administer oaths and affirmations, and to perform such other acts as are allowed or required by law.

notary stamp or seal. A device used by a notary that makes an imprint or embossment.

oath. A notarial act in which a notary certifies that a person made a vow or affirmation including reference to a Supreme Being in the presence of the notary. "Do you swear that the information you give concerning this writing is the truth, so help you, God?"

official act. An act performed by a qualified person appointed or elected to serve the public.

official misconduct. (1) A notary's performance of a prohibited act or failure to perform a mandated act as set forth in N.C. General Statute Chapter 10A or any other law in connection with notarization. (2) The performance of a notarial act in a manner found by the Secretary of State to be negligent or against the public interest.

personal knowledge of identity. Familiarity with an individual gained through interactions with that individual over a period of time and sufficient to eliminate every reasonable doubt that the individual has the identity claimed.

resignation. The formal statement of one's intention to terminate an appointment and cease performing the duties of the office.

revoke. To terminate a person's commission or appointment prior to its normal expiration. The Department of the Secretary of State has the authority to revoke notaries' public commissions in North Carolina.

satisfactory evidence of identity. Identification of an individual based on either of the following: (1) one current document issued by a federal or state government and including the individual's photograph or (2) identification by a credible person personally known to the notary and having personal knowledge of the individual's identity.

Secretary. The Secretary of State.

signature of notary public. A notary must sign the name under which he or she was commissioned and no other.

term. The maximum time for which an elected or appointed office may be held without re-election or reappointment. (North Carolina notaries public have a term of five years.)

title. Proof or evidence of ownership of property.

transaction. An act or agreement made between two or more entities.

transfer. To transmit the possession or control, especially of title to property, from one entity to another.

venue. The part of a notary certificate providing the location in which the notarial act was performed.

verification or proof. A notarial act in which a notary certifies that a signer, whose identity is personally known to the notary or proven on the basis of satisfactory evidence, has, in the notary's presence, voluntarily signed a document and taken an oath or affirmation concerning the document.

witness. A person who observes an event.

Glossary provided by The Notary Public Section of the North Carolina Department of the Secretary of State.

Some definitions taken from Raymond C. Rothman, *Notary Public Practices & Glossary*, the National Notary Association, 1978. Used with permission of the National Notary Association, 9350 De Soto Ave., Chatsworth, CA 91311-4926, and reprinted with permission. Contact the NNA at 1-800-876-6827 or view their Web site at www.nationalnotary.org.

Appendix IV

Frequently Asked Questions

1. Are applicants for *reappointment* required to have an elected official recommend them, by signature, to the Department of the Secretary of State?

   No. This statutory requirement was deleted effective October 1, 1995.

2. Is the green transmittal letter received with the last appointment valid as a reappointment form?

   No. The notary must obtain the current required statutory reappointment application.

3. How much is the fee for reappointment?

   The nonrefundable fee is $50.00, payable as a check or money order. Cash will be accepted only if presented in person.

4. Does the secretary of state remind notaries when commissions must be renewed?

   No. It is the notary's responsibility to obtain the proper form.

5. Can a notary be commissioned in the county in which he or she works if he or she resides in a different North Carolina county?

   No. A commission is issued in the county in which the notary works only when the applicant resides outside North Carolina.

6. Must a notary have the latest edition of the *Notary Public Guidebook* to qualify for reappointment?

   No, but the Department recommends a current edition be purchased because expectations and law concerning notary practice change.

7. **When notarizing a vehicle title, should the notary charge the fees set by Chapter 10A or those charged by the DMV?**

    North Carolina notaries public charge the fees set by G. S. Chapter 10A. Tag agents in DMV offices charge the fees set by G.S. 20-42, which also gives the DMV the authority to administer oaths and certify copies of records.

8. **When a vehicle title is being notarized, do both the purchaser and seller have to be in the notary's presence?**

    For Section A of the titles, only the seller must be present. For Section B, only the purchaser must be present.

    There are several title forms in use by the DMV. Notaries should be aware of the following:

    —Older vehicle title documents have the words: "Subscribed and sworn to before me in my presence...." New vehicle title documents do not. If the oath language is on the document, an oath is required to be administered to the individual signing the document.

    —A new vehicle title document (MVR 191 [Form I in Chapter IV of this book]) was developed by the Department of Transportation effective November 1, 2001. Notaries public need to be cautious in acknowledging these documents as follows:

      —The venue statements are no longer on the MVR 191 as amended. A notary public will not have to enter the county and state in which the acknowledgment was taken.

      —There are name and signature lines for various persons above the notarial certificates. To keep with long-standing practice in North Carolina, a notary should cross out any blank lines above his or her signature before completing the acknowledgment.

      —The space on the new form for a notary's seal or stamp is very small. A notary should ensure that his or her seal or stamp is readable in its entirety and that it does not obscure any words in the certificate.

    If a notary public performs a notarial act on the new MVR 191, he or she risks violating the Notary Act. On the other hand, if the notary complies with the Notary Act in all respects while he or she notarizes the document, the notary may void the title entirely. Therefore the Department of the Secretary of State recommends that notaries send individuals seeking notarization on the MVR 191 to the nearest DMV tag agent office to obtain this service.

9. **What must a notary do if he or she changes his or her name?**

    Complete and file a name change form within thirty days of the change.

10. **Can a notary notarize documents while he or she is waiting for his or her name change application to be processed? If so, how does the notary sign his or her name?**

Yes, the notary can notarize documents during this time. He or she should sign the documents as previously commissioned until he or she receives notification to take the oath of office (green sheet) from the Department. The notary should then abstain from performing any notarial act until he or she takes the oath at a register of deeds office and obtains a new seal with the new name.

11. **What should a notary do if he or she changes *both* his or her county of residence and name during the term of the commission?**

Reapply for a new commission by submitting a reappointment application.

12. **How can a notary learn about statutory changes that affect notary practice?**

By contacting The Notary Public Section, the county register of deeds office, or a local community college, or by consulting the secretary of state's Web site (http://www.sosnc.com/) or the North Carolina General Statutes.

13. **Is it the notary's responsibility to add a certificate to a document if one is needed?**

No, it is the responsibility of the creator of the document, but the notary may add a certificate according to his or her judgment.

14. **If a certificate is added to a document, what elements must be included?**

All statutory forms for the certification of acknowledgement or proof of written instruments must include
    —the name of the state and county in which the certification occurs;
    —the body of the certificate, stating before whom, by whom, and in what manner the signature was acknowledged or proved;
    —the date of the acknowledgement or proof; and
    —the signature and seal of the officer who took the acknowledgement or proof.

15. **Can a notary certify a true copy of a document?**

No. G.S. 10A-9(a)(1-3) does not give notaries the authority to create and/or sign any statement of certification of a true copy.

16. **What are the notary's responsibilities in the proper attestation of a signature?**

Notaries should remember the acronym CPRE when attesting a signature.
—Clear and legible impression of stamp or seal
—Proper signature
—Readable appearance of notary's name
—Expiration date of notary's commission
If the document to be notarized does not contain any language for an acknowledgement, oath or affirmation, or verification or proof, such language *must* be added before the document can be properly notarized. A document containing an attestation without the appropriate language is *not* properly notarized.

17. **If a commission was originally issued under a nickname, does the notary have to change the commission to his or her legal name?**

No. If the *original* commission was issued prior to October 1991, he or she may continue to use the nickname. If the change of name resulted from marriage or a legal change of name, the commission must be issued in the correct, legal name and a new seal must be purchased.

18. **If an applicant has been convicted of a felony, can he or she become a notary?**

No. Unless his or her rights have been restored, a felon is constitutionally barred from holding public office. Being a notary public is considered a public office.

19. **If a notary, while commissioned, is convicted of any felony or other crime involving dishonesty or moral turpitude, what should he or she do?**

The notary should immediately stop acting as a notary and notify The Notary Public Section. In most instances the notary will be given the opportunity to resign his or her commission in lieu of revocation.

20. **How far in advance can a notary apply for reappointment?**

Thirty days before his or her commission expires.

21. **If a notary resides in one county, can he or she notarize a document in another county? If so, what county does the notary use on the heading of the acknowledgment?**

Yes, the notary may notarize documents in any county in North Carolina. The county used in the heading is the county in which the acknowledgment is taken.

22. **Does a notary have to be sworn in upon each reappointment to office?**

Yes.

23. **If a notary does not appear before the register of deeds for commission within ninety days of the effective date of the commission, what happens?**

The register of deeds returns the notary certificate and transmittal letter to the Department of the Secretary of State and the applicant must reapply and repay the application fee.

24. **In what capacity can military personnel act as North Carolina notaries?**

Persons authorized to act as notaries by 10 U.S.C. § 1044a may perform notarial acts only for certain categories of military personnel mentioned in that statute. In doing so they are *not* acting as North Carolina notaries since their authority is derived from federal rather than state law. If they wish, they may apply for a North Carolina notary commission.

25. **Where can the *Notary Public Guidebook* be purchased?**

The Institute of Government (CB #3330 Knapp-Sanders Building, UNC Chapel Hill, Chapel Hill, NC 27599-3330; 919-966-4119; http://sog.unc.edu/) or your local community college bookstore.

26. **How long does it take to process a notary application?**

Three weeks, if the application is complete and correct.

27. **If I notarize a document, can I witness it as well?**

No.

28. **How does a notary properly notarize a document for an elderly person who lacks the customary proper identification?**

A credible person known to the notary can verify the identity of the person.

29. **Can a notary take an acknowledgment by phone or fax?**

No.

30. **Can a notary acknowledge two signatures if only one of the signers is present?**

No.

31. **Is a notary responsible for the proper completion of a vehicle title when notarizing the title?**

The notary must ensure that the document is complete *above* the notarial certificate before performing a notarial act. (See also Question 8 above.)

32. **Is the notary responsible for putting a lien on a car?**

No.

33. **How much can a notary charge for a verification or proof, since the notary is both witnessing a signature and giving an oath?**

A notary may charge $3.00 per signature for taking and certifying the acknowledgment for the execution of any instrument or writing, $3.00 per person for administering oaths or affirmations without verification or proof, and $3.00 per signature for a verification or proof.

34. **Can a notary notarize a vehicle title for his or her spouse?**

Yes, if the notary is not a named party on the title or an interested party to the transaction. The Department highly recommends, however, that notaries not perform notarial acts for relatives.

35. **What is the procedure for notarizing the signature of a person who cannot write but who signs with a mark?**

The notary uses the same procedure as for a personal appearance. The mark is considered a signature in North Carolina.

This list was provided by The Notary Public Section of the North Carolina Department of the Secretary of State.